THE HOLY WEEK

Experience the Teachings and Miracles of Jesus Christ's Final Week

ROB SHALLENBERGER

THE HOLY WEEK:
Experience the Teachings and Miracles
of Jesus Christ's Final Week

© **Copyright 2022 by Star Leadership LLC**

Cover Design By: David Christenson
Cover Art By: Karl Bloch

All Rights Reserved.

ISBN: 9780988845992

CONTENTS

INTRODUCTION:

IMAGINE YOU WERE THERE

testify that Jesus Christ is the promised Messiah and that He is our resurrected Lord.

And I'm not alone; many theological and scholarly books about the life of Jesus testify, in great detail, to His messiahship and resurrection. This book, however, takes a different approach – a personal approach. Rather than debate the merits of a specific date or interpretation of scripture, this book invites you to *experience* what it must have been like to be with Jesus and His disciples during His final week.

The primary objective of this book is for you to *have a revelatory experience* by visualizing and deeply pondering each event that Jesus and those around Him experienced during the week of His death and resurrection, commonly known as the Holy Week.

Many are familiar with the story of Jesus' final week on a surface level. Matthew, Mark, Luke, and John each captured certain aspects from their point of view, but it can often be challenging to piece them all together. I'll draw on each of their accounts, as well as other life experiences and research, to make it easier for you to envision each experience. The chapters are intentionally short to be used as a guide for your quiet contemplation.

With this book, I invite you to step back in history, 2000 years ago, and imagine being there. Walk alongside Jesus and his friends – see what they saw, smell what they smelled, and experience the tears and laughter they experienced. At the end of each chapter, I encourage you to pause, contemplate, and pray about what you've just read. By doing so, I hope you connect with Him on a deeper and more meaningful level and open doors for new revelation that makes each story personal to you. I think you might be surprised by what the Lord can teach you beyond just reading alone.

The key to getting the most out of this book is to visualize yourself in each situation and shift from *reading* to *experiencing*.

Visualize

While you read, take yourself to that event in your mind's eye and visualize being present in the moment. Try to involve all five senses and immerse yourself in the sights, sounds, and smells.

For example, Mark tells us that Jesus rode into Jerusalem on a donkey a week before His crucifixion (Mark 11:7). That's where most people stop—the historical fact. But can you visualize being there, walking beside Him, listening to the crowd shout "Hosanna, to the Son of David!"? Can you see His followers fervently waving branches in adoration and acknowledgment of the return of the Messiah? Can you see His tear-streaked cheeks as He paused to overlook the city of Jerusalem?

That was just one example, but imagine being there for all the events during His final week. This approach differentiates between reading a historical fact and making it come alive and personal.

There is a saying: Before assuming you know someone, "walk a mile in their shoes." By visualizing these events and making them personal, you will come close to walking a mile in their shoes. As a result of this personal approach, you will know Peter, John, Mary Magdalene, and many other disciples much better. More importantly, you will *know* and *appreciate* Jesus on another level because you have *experienced* the life-changing events of His final week

Ponder and Pray

Once you have visualized being there, take some time to pause, ponder, and pray about what you experienced.

Many in our culture have lost the ability to quiet our minds and ponder. Running in the hamster wheel of life, we rarely take the time to be still. Yet, we greatly enhance our capacity to receive personal revelation and have sacred experiences when we learn to be still and listen. The scriptures even tell us to be still and know God (Psalm 40:10) and to be still and wait patiently for the Lord (Psalm 37:7).

John 17:3 states, "And this is life eternal, that they might **know** thee the only true God, and Jesus Christ, whom thou hast sent" (emphasis mine). The invitation in this book isn't to know *about* Him; it's to *know* Him through experience and personal revelation. Quieting our minds, visualizing, pondering, and praying is the best way to prepare our hearts and minds to receive revelation so that we might *know* Him on a deeper level.

Visualizing the intimate experiences and pondering about the events of His final week will draw you into a closer relationship with Him. When was the last time you, your spouse, or a close friend experienced an exciting or dangerous event together? Didn't you feel a new connection to that person afterward and spend the following hours or days reflecting on how awesome, dangerous, or exciting the event was? The experience and reflection bonded you closer together. If you visualize yourself with Jesus during His final days, it will be like the two of you experiencing all the suspense, trauma, and pain together. Then, as you ponder and pray about it in the following days, you will establish a closer bond with Him as your personal Savior.

For some people, pondering comes easy. However, others may not know how to quiet their minds and listen. For this reason, I've provided questions at the end of each chapter to get you started. You might take a couple of minutes to ponder those questions, or maybe you take twenty minutes or more – it truly depends on you and your situation. I also encourage you to have a journal handy to write down your answers and other thoughts or ideas.

The events surrounding the crucifixion and resurrection have always been very personal to me. Over the years, as I read and pondered these scriptures, I increasingly pictured myself there as one of His disciples. Each time, I felt like the Lord was teaching and showing me something new and different. This doesn't make me a biblical scholar, an expert, or anyone extra special, but it revealed to me how the Lord speaks to each of us in unique and personal ways. That was my motivation for setting out to write this book – not to impart my knowledge or revelation, but to help set the stage for you to receive whatever personal and unique revelation the Lord wants to show you.

The Layout

The book is divided into two sections. Part One describes the events leading up to the Last Supper. Part Two covers the Last Supper to His Resurrection.

Each chapter is essential. But, if you're on the go and only have time to read a few chapters initially, make sure you read the critical chapters from Part Two – the Last Supper to His Resurrection. These are the life-changing events that transformed the world. I'm confident that once you read these chapters, you will return shortly to read the ones you missed.

Each chapter also has a specific flow and layout:

1. **A description of the actual event.** Each chapter will summarize what happened from the combined perspective of the various gospels and include my descriptions, analysis, and experiences to help paint a full and enlivened picture. As you read, immerse yourself and imagine being *present* with the Lord.

2. **Gospel references**. At the end of each chapter, you will find the scriptural references from the gospels that describe the event. It will be a more enriched experience if you take the time to read these accounts. In this way, treat the book as a study guide.

3. **Prophetic references.** Following the gospel accounts are the prophetic references. The last days of Jesus had been prophesied and written about by certain prophets for thousands of years. These references will help you see clearly how Jesus fulfilled all the messianic prophesies.

4. **Ponder, Visualize and Personalize**. This section is where I ask you questions to help stimulate contemplation. Use these prompts to focus on the individual events and imagine experiencing them. These questions will help you reflect on how the actions of Jesus – His human pain and suffering and His divine redemption – are applicable in your life today.

Some of you may not be completely familiar with the scripture references or theological concepts I present. That's ok! I primarily use the King James Version of the Bible (KJV), and references are included in the text for you to look up easily. Additionally, I quote from the "Doctrine and Covenants" (D&C) and other prophetic books read by the Church of Jesus Christ of Latter-Day Saints. That doesn't mean that this book is only for members of the Church of Jesus Christ. It's for everyone, even if you are not of the Christian faith. After all, what you are about to read was done for all humanity!

By reading this book, and the personal experiences it hopefully generates, I hope you will forever look at the final week of Christ's life in a new and personal light. Consider reviewing these events and what you have written in your journal annually, especially during the Holy Week, and share these experiences with your family and friends.

Then, when you read the New Testament, approach Easter Sunday, or merely talk about the Holy Week, it will be different because you've *experienced* it. Your insight will be deeper and richer.

Finally, I hope this approach of personalizing and visualizing each event will move you forward on your journey to *know* Jesus Christ and not just know *about* Him!

PART ONE

BETHANY TO THE CONFRONTATION

CHAPTER 1:

THE ANOINTING IN BETHANY

J esus resided primarily in Bethany during His final visit to Jerusalem until He was betrayed in Gethsemane. Bethany was a town approximately two miles from Jerusalem near the southeastern slope of the Mount of Olives.

According to Mathew and John, Jesus was anointed in Bethany at the house of Simon the leper six days before Passover. The anointing is one of those events surrounded by varying opinions about whether there was one anointing, multiple anointings, and on which day it occurred. Rather than worry about the exact timing, I want to focus here on the experience itself. Mary, the sister of Martha and Lazarus, anointed Him. She used Nard (Spikenard), a rare ointment from the Himalayas worth approximately 300 Denarii (nearly a year's wage for the average Jew). This costly ointment would only be reserved for anointing a king or royal priest.

The gospel accounts mentioned that Jesus, Mary, Lazarus, and other disciples, gathered around a table at Simon's house for supper, indicating that it was likely late afternoon or evening.

Jesus recently raised Lazarus from the dead. This miracle was a big deal, and it's easy to see how news like that would spread like wildfire. John 12:9 mentioned: "Much people of the Jews therefore knew that he [Jesus] was there: and they came not for Jesus' sake only, but that they might see Lazarus also, whom he had raised from the dead." This passage conveys that people were just as eager to see Lazarus as they were to see Jesus. So, it's no surprise that a crowd soon followed when Jesus showed up at Simon's house, especially considering that Lazarus was there.

The Anointing

Picture being in the room among the crowd at Simon's house. Visualize a group – Jesus, Lazarus, Mary among them – sitting on cushions around the table. Imagine additional people lining the room's walls, including Judas and some of the disciples. You would likely see the flicker of candles while the fading sunlight peeked through the windows. Now, picture Mary as she kneels in front of Jesus and opens the ointment. Think about her taking His feet into her hands and using her dark hair to gently wipe the Spikenard on His feet. The room would have been filled with woody, spicy, and musty aromas (John 12:3). Imagine smelling these rich aromas, as well as the food and the slight char of smoke that would have touched the air while they cooked. Finally, picture how the Savior looked lovingly into Mary's eyes. It must have been a sacred and tender moment.

Some were in awe of what they saw. Others were furious that this expensive ointment was being "wasted" on Him rather than sold and the proceeds given to the poor. The noted critic was Judas, who was already conspiring to betray Jesus. Envision Judas with the other disciples around the room, talking in a displeasing tone. Imagine how those side discussions distracted others at the table from this tender moment between Mary and Jesus. I wonder if Mary could overhear what they were saying and how she might have felt as their voices floated across the room. Picture Jesus looking up from Mary, His eyes searching the room until they landed on his followers with a frustrated look on His face. He collectively rebuked them, saying, "Let her alone; why trouble ye her? She hath wrought a good work on me. For ye have the poor with you always, and whensoever ye will ye may do them good; but me ye have not always. She hath done what she could: she is come aforehand to anoint my body to the burying" (Mark 14:6–8).

It appeared this rebuke was the straw that broke the camel's back for Judas. He then left the house and sought an opportunity to betray Jesus and deliver Him to the chief priests, selling his soul for thirty pieces of silver.

Imagine, after that gentle rebuke, Jesus turning back to Mary to encourage her. Picture Him touching her gently on the shoulder while still holding the gaze of those in the room. I think any embarrassment Mary might have felt would have dissolved in his following statement. Jesus told those still gathered in the room that future generations would remember her for this memorial and anointing. "Wheresoever this gospel shall be preached throughout the whole world, this also that she hath done shall be spoken of for a memorial of her" (Mark 14:9).

Reference Scriptures

John 12:1–8

Mathew 26:1–13

John 11:55

Mark 14:1–9

Ponder, Visualize, and Personalize

Take a few minutes to imagine being in the room with Jesus, Mary, Martha, Lazarus, and the others. While you think about it and answer the questions below, capture any thoughts or feelings in a journal.

1. Have you ever been part of an intimate or sacred, yet public, experience with a crowd of people?

2. How have you truly honored someone in your life?

3. What have you sacrificed or consecrated for the Lord? (Clearly, something valued at 300 denarii was a big sacrifice for Mary). How did Christ accept or acknowledge your offering?

4. Did you ask Him how He felt about it? If not, ask Him!

CHAPTER 2:

THE TRIUMPHAL ENTRY INTO JERUSALEM

Shortly after His anointing in Bethany, Jesus entered Jerusalem to prepare for the forthcoming Passover feast. How awesome would it have been to watch Jesus, the King of Kings, make his triumphal entry into Jerusalem on a donkey? Mathew, Mark, Luke, and John presented four different accounts of this event. Each brought a unique perspective by noting common events from that day and highlighting specific details that the other authors omitted or missed. But unfortunately, many of the disciples didn't realize the significance of what they were experiencing until after His death.

Like many other things Jesus did, this entrance to Jerusalem was rich in symbolism. So much of His entry was rooted in His kingship and sacrifice as the paschal lamb.

Three elements of symbolism are essential to note before describing the actual entry.

First, riding on a donkey was a symbol of peace. Jesus came in peace rather than riding on a horse, which most warriors, conquerors, or kings would have ridden. Ironically, when He returns the second time, He will be on a white horse returning as the true King of Kings to claim His earth as the rightful heir (Revelation 6:2 and 19:11,14). By riding on a donkey, He fulfilled the prophetic statement in Zechariah 9:9:

See, your King comes to you, righteous and having salvation, gentle and riding on a donkey, on a colt, the foal of a donkey. I will take away the chariots from Ephraim and the war-horses from Jerusalem, and the battle bow will be broken. He will proclaim peace to the nations.

In addition, Jacob spoke Messianically about the specific symbolism of the donkey when blessing Judah. In Genesis 49:11, he said:

Binding his foal unto the vine, and his ass's colt unto the choice vine; he washed his garments in wine, and clothes in the blood of the grapes.

Second, by lineage, Jesus was the rightful King of the Jews. Had the Romans not occupied Jerusalem, He would have had a legal claim to be the rightful King through the Davidic line. How fitting that the rightful King of the Jews entered with the people shouting praises to the "Son of David" – a title only used for King Solomon and the promised Messiah.

Third, on Sunday (the first day of the week), people would have been in the process of bringing the paschal lambs from Bethlehem and the surrounding area to Jerusalem in preparation for Passover and their sacrifice. It's fitting that Jesus, the perfect lamb of God, would have been entering Jerusalem simultaneously in preparation for His sacrifice – the real sacrifice.

Now to the actual experience of His entry.

The Triumphal Entry

Nearly all scholars agree that His entrance happened on Sunday, known today as Palm Sunday. Jesus and His followers left His temporary residence in Bethany, and when they approached Bethphage, a place near the Mount of Olives, He sent two of his disciples to a nearby village to get an ass (donkey) and her colt. Knowing someone would question His disciples, Jesus told them, "If any man say ought unto you [asks what you're doing], ye shall say, The Lord hath need of them; and straightway he will send them" (Matthew 21:3). And so it was. Someone asked the two disciples what they were doing, and they relayed Jesus' instructions. The unnamed person allowed the disciples to take the donkeys without further questions.

When the two disciples arrived at where Jesus and the others waited, they put their clothes on the donkey, and Jesus climbed its back.

When Jesus faced Jerusalem and proceeded toward the city, He knew exactly what he was doing. Isaiah 50:7 says: "Therefore have I set my face like a flint, and I know that I shall not be ashamed." He set his face like flint – in other words, he was resolute, focused, and expected opposition – and was not ashamed.

Several of the Apostles noted that a "very great multitude" of people gathered because they knew Jesus was coming (as well as the miracle man Lazarus). In today's language, they said, "There was a huge crowd." Many people gathered in the swelling crowd to see both Jesus and Lazarus. Some came from the local area, and others were there to celebrate Passover. During Passover, it was common for the population to surge from the typical 20,000 – 40,000 people to upwards of more than 250,000 people. Suffice it to say, the ordinarily small city of Jerusalem was very congested at Passover.

When Jesus approached the city, the very great multitude "spread their garments in the way; others cut down branches from trees and strawed them in the way" (Mathew 21:8). Both the garments laid on the ground and the waving of palm branches were gestures acknowledging Jesus as King of Israel, and, more specifically, as the Messiah.

The multitude then cried: "Hosanna to the Son of David: Blessed is he that cometh in the name of the Lord; Hosanna to the highest" (Matthew 21:9). I've seen videos portraying His entry where people gently waved palm leaves, talked in hushed tones, and it was all presented as a very passive event. When I read words like "cried" and "shouted," I interpret this as no passive event; this was a dramatic experience that people discussed for subsequent generations. The crowd was big enough, and the scene was dramatic enough that "the city was moved," and people asked, "who is this?" Even the present Pharisees noted, "the world is gone after him" (John 12:19).

Imagine being in the crowd and feeling the energy that must have been there – watching the people take off their shawls or coverings and excitedly laying them on the ground in front of the approaching donkey. Picture being there alongside those who waved palm branches as Jesus peacefully approached. What an incredible experience it would have been. There was likely a faint smell of smoke in the air that would have been common because of the many outdoor stoves and fires. It was probably loud because of all the people near the city gate and the commotion from the various groups.

There were undoubtedly many people struggling to get close to Jesus – to hear Him, see Him, and touch Him. Many recognized Jesus as the Messiah and saw Him coming to take his rightful place as King. The laying of their clothes and the waving of the palm branches was their acknowledgment of who He was. Since the recent raising of Lazarus, combined with His many other miracles, many people were excited that the Messiah finally came to overthrow the Romans. However, most still didn't understand the role of the Messiah and what His intent was. Think of the anticipation, the excitement, and especially the feelings you might have felt when He rode by and momentarily locked eyes with you. What a scene that must have been!

When the Pharisees heard the people yelling Hosanna and waving palm branches, they said to Jesus, "rebuke thy disciples" (Luke 19:39). His response to the Pharisees was powerful and telling. "I tell you that, if these [the people] should hold their peace, the stones would immediately cry out" (Luke 19:40).

Think about the power in that statement. Jesus, the creator of the earth, knew that even nature would praise Him if man failed. Jesus went like a lamb to the slaughter. If the people didn't acknowledge Him and praise Him, the elements of His creation, such as the rocks, would still have picked up the praise in their stead.

When Jesus came near the city, the weight of the moment must have settled on him because He lamented and even wept, saying:

> If thou hadst known, even thou, at least in this thy day, the things which belong unto thy peace! But now they are hid from thine eyes. For the days shall come upon thee, that thine enemies shall cast a trench about thee, and compass thee round, and keep thee in on every side. And shall lay thee even with the ground, and thy children within thee; and they shall not leave in thee one stone upon another; because thou knewest not the time of thy visitation (Luke 19:42–44).

From the disciples' perspective, this must have been a sacred moment that filled them with wonder. In the gospels, Mathew, Mark, Luke, and John each recalled His triumphal entry differently by highlighting specific details. Imagine if you were one of them escorting Jesus on the donkey through the crowds of people. Envision being there when He paused to look up at the walled city of Jerusalem, tears streaming down His cheeks, and hearing Him lament its future. Imagine the mixed emotions you probably would have seen in His eyes and on His face at that moment and the powerful sense of love and sadness in His voice while He wept.

But not everyone saw the arrival of Jesus as a sacred moment. From the perspective of the religious leadership, they must have been enraged because Jesus had just issued a veiled threat promising the destruction of their most holy building – the Temple ("...and they shall not leave in thee one stone upon another"). Interestingly, that prophetic statement was fulfilled seventy years later when the Romans laid waste to Jerusalem and destroyed the Temple.

The triumphal entry of Jesus into Jerusalem would have been one of the most amazing moments this world had ever seen. After being anointed in Bethany, Jesus peacefully approached the place where He would offer Himself up as the unblemished lamb later that week!

Reference Scriptures

John 12:12-19
Mathew 21:1-11
Luke 19:29-44
Mark 11:1-10

Prophetic References

Zechariah 9:9
Genesis 49:11

Ponder, Visualize, and Personalize

Take a few minutes to visualize and experience what it might have been like to be there for Jesus' majestic, humble entry into Jerusalem. Then, while you think about that and the questions below, capture any thoughts or feelings in a journal.

1. Is there a time in your life when you felt so moved that you wanted to shout out in praise something like "Hosanna to the highest?"

2. If so, what was that experience, and how would you describe your feelings?

CHAPTER 3:

THE TEMPLE CLEANSING

Why include the temple cleansing as one of the significant events from His final week? And why did this matter so much to Jesus? Why make such a big scene? The answer, I believe, lies in the important lessons we can learn from these experiences.

After Jesus' dramatic entrance into Jerusalem, messianic expectations among His followers were at a fever pitch. However, the outward proclamations of the crowd that Jesus was the Messiah, and Jesus' own self-assurance, set Him on a collision course with the Sanhedrin and other Jewish leaders. They had their eyes on Him; He was a marked man, and His disciples must have thought it risky going to the Temple after the commotion of His triumphal entry. And yet, Jesus went anyways, and by doing so, walked into the proverbial hornet's nest and hit it with a stick!

The Temple

It's important to note that scholars still debate whether there were one or two temple cleansings.

Matthew, Mark, and Luke recorded the second cleansing, but not John. There are differences between the two events, aside from being three years apart. In the first cleansing, temple officials confronted Jesus immediately (John 2:18), whereas, in the second cleansing, they confronted Him the following day (Matthew 21:17 – 23). In the first event, Jesus made a whip of cords to drive out the sellers, but there is no mention of a whip in the second cleansing.

If there were two cleansings, I wonder how many money changers, merchants, and onlookers remembered Him from the beginning of His ministry three years prior. When Jesus wants to drive a point home, He clearly knows how. But whether there were one or two cleansings isn't the focus; the point here is to focus on the experience.

Before we get into the details of what happened, it's helpful to understand the context of this fiery event.

First, Judea was under the rule of the Romans, which meant that the people used Roman coins. However, Jewish law required a half-shekel coin for a tribute to the service of the Temple (a temple tax). Therefore, the outer area of the Temple became a convenient place where people could exchange the Roman coin for the Tyrian shekel – which was used like the half-shekel to pay the temple tax. When you do the math, tens of thousands of visitors for the Passover sacrifice was a giant money-making machine for the Sanhedrin.

Second, the Temple complex was estimated to hold up to 75,000 people. The entire Temple Mount consisted of three different courts. The outer court was a large open-air square commonly referred to as the Court of the Gentiles. This was the closest point to the actual Temple where non-Jewish visitors could gather, including the non-Jewish believers in Jesus. Next was a small courtyard where Jewish men and women could enter. Proceeding inward was the next court, where only men were allowed. Finally, the Holy of Holies was the small, innermost court where only priests could enter.

The money-changers and merchants set up their businesses in the Court of the Gentiles. Because it was challenging for many people to bring the required animal sacrifices, these merchants developed a lucrative business selling birds, cattle, and sheep. The temple visitors didn't like these merchants because they charged exorbitant prices. These merchants, however, occupied the *only* place where the Gentiles could worship the living God at the Temple. The Jewish nation was supposed to be a light to other nations but instead acted as a stumbling block for the Gentiles coming to worship God during one of their largest celebrations.

The merchants, and the priests who allowed them to be there, appeared to care nothing for true worship as long as they could make money and keep up the rituals. It was evident that Jesus loathed this sacrilege, which kept the nations from learning about the living God in His sanctuary.

Two things about this ritual angered the Lord:

1. *The chosen location for setting up shop.* The merchants had turned the sacred Temple – the house of the Lord – into a filthy business. Instead of a house of worship, it became a profit center for those who sold animals and exchanged money.

2. *The oppression of the poor.* It's not that exchanging money for a small profit was inherently wrong; it's that it often

became a way to gouge and oppress the poor. For example, pilgrims rarely brought their animals and were therefore forced to pay exorbitant prices to purchase an animal to sacrifice. In addition, these merchants leveraged Passover and the Lord's house to make a handsome profit and oppress those who already struggled to make ends meet.

With that brief context in mind, let's get into how Jesus responded – the cleansing of the temple.

The Temple Cleansing

Imagine when Jesus, with His followers, ascended the steps and entered the Court of the Gentiles. He anticipated what He would see and was likely already upset. Can you see yourself standing beside Him overlooking the courtyard, with the Temple looming above the outer walls? Picture the hustle and bustle of the people tightly packed into the square, finally ready to offer their sacrifice after a long journey. Think about the smell that emanated from the thousands of people who hadn't bathed in several days, plus the animals, their blood and entrails, and their dung. There must have been all kinds of potent smells in the courtyard.

Imagine the hundreds of loud conversations and negotiations you would see between the pilgrims and the vendors. Then, visualize yourself standing next to Jesus, seeing the flame in His eyes as they swept over the courtyard. His eyes would likely have conveyed that He was ready to clean house – literally!

These merchants were desecrating His house, and He was clearly infuriated. His followers likely wondered what He would do next. Imagine Jesus walking resolutely to the nearest table, grabbing the side, and throwing it over. Picture the shocked look on the face of the money changer, wondering what was going on while coins danced in the air and sprawled out on the stone floor. Next, envision the people near the tables spinning around, anxious to see the commotion and realizing they should probably get out of the way. Finally, imagine Jesus breathing heavily, moving to the subsequent tables, and flipping them over as well. I expect many conversations stopped when the people realized something big was happening.

At this point, visualize the crowd receding away from the heated exchange between Jesus and the vendors, fearful of getting caught between them. Some would have recognized Jesus as the Messiah; others must have wondered who He was and what He was doing. Regardless, it would make sense that the crowd would side with Jesus and cheer Him on, knowing these money changers were there to pillage them.

With the crowd cheering Him on in the background, imagine Jesus, dressed in a simple tunic, pointing to the Temple, rebuking the merchants with a loud voice:

It is written, My house shall be called the house of prayer; but ye have made it a den of thieves (Matthew 21:12-13).

Or, as Mark said:

Is it not written, My house shall be called a house of prayer for the nations? But you have made it a den of robbers (Mark 11:17).

Think about what you would have felt from the perspective of the money changers and vendors. First, I wonder if they thought, "Who is this guy?" Then, as Jesus continued to overturn the tables, and it was apparent the crowd supported Him, they probably thought, "I'm out of here."

What would you have felt from a disciple's perspective? I could only imagine His disciples felt a bursting sense of pride and awe when they watched Jesus take ownership of the Temple and do what so many people wanted to see done – drive out the corrupt merchants. They were probably a little on edge and worried as well, looking over their shoulders, wondering when the authorities would show up to arrest them.

I'm sure the inferred ownership wasn't lost on the Sadducees or other Jewish leaders when Jesus called the Temple *His* house. Here Jesus was, in the very area over which the Sanhedrin claimed supreme jurisdiction, and He was claiming it as *His* house! Yet, with thousands of people surrounding Him, cheering Him on, and the merchants running, the Sanhedrin were powerless to touch Him.

Thus, we see the righteous indignation of Jesus as the Son of God. He turned over the money changers' tables and drove the merchants out. The very nation that was to be a blessing to the world was not allowing the world to be blessed. Jesus couldn't let that pass without a strong rebuke.

Compassion and Healing

After Jesus had turned over the last table in the Court of the Gentiles, picture a large crowd encircling Him in anxious anticipation of what He might do next. Imagine Jesus looking into the people's eyes, sweat covering his face, and His chest heaving up and down from all the energy spent. The awe-struck crowd approached closer to Him, more convinced than ever that He was the Messiah. Then, in a significant change of mood and emotion, Jesus compassionately beckoned the crowd even closer to heal them. Imagine Jesus extending His arms to the crowd in a welcoming gesture, inviting the children and any who were sick to come forward:

> And the blind and the lame came to him in the temple; and he healed them. And when the chief priests and scribes saw the wonderful things that he did, and the children crying in the temple, and saying, Hosanna to the Son of David; they [the chief priests and Sadducees] were sore displeased (Matthew 21:14-15).

What an incredible scene this must have been. In the recently cleansed Court of the Gentiles, Jesus, the promised Messiah, healed the lame to walk and the blind to receive sight. Even the children cried, "Hosanna to the Son of David!" How could someone not believe it? Yet, the temple priests were incensed because He wiped out their money machine and took ownership of *their* building. Yet, again, they were powerless to take Him because the people couldn't get enough of what they were experiencing and crowded around Him.

It was one thing to see the incredible power of Jesus overturning the tables and driving the merchants out of the court. But to witness the loving, tender miracles that followed was even more remarkable. Imagine seeing the look on the face of the person who just received sight for the first time. Picture seeing someone rise up and walk after being lame their entire life. Think about how these people would have looked at Jesus after He healed them. Finally, visualize how the crowd would have responded to these miracles – their expressions and conversations, the murmuring, the laughter, the tears, the shouts of joy. I envision this crowd with mouths draped open, cheering on the people who just received their sight and newfound ability to walk. What an incredible swing of emotions the crowd must have experienced. In this context, it's easier to understand why this intense and emotionally charged experience was included in the gospels.

Among the many lessons from this amazing experience, here are just four:

1. Don't trifle with sacred things. In the Temple, Jesus reminded us that God will not be mocked.

2. Even though the Lord is filled with love, He will not tolerate it when people mock sacred things or defile that which is holy.

3. The Temple is the house of God. He clearly loved the Temple and visited it often.

4. Jesus experienced emotions as well. In this case, He was angry with the people who desecrated His Father's house, used it as a place for gain, and oppressed the poor. Yet, once cleansed, He immediately turned to the people and lovingly healed them.

Reference Scriptures

Mathew 21:12-17

Luke 19:45-48

Mark 11:15-19

Ponder, Visualize, and Personalize

Take a few minutes to visualize being in the Court of the Gentiles. What would it have been like to witness the significant events from that day? Then, while you think about that and the questions below, capture any thoughts or feelings in a journal.

1. Have you ever been in a situation where you felt the need to stand up for what was right, even when it might have been embarrassing?

2. Have you ever witnessed someone else stand up for what is right or the truth? How did you feel as you watched them?

3. How might you have felt – as one of the disciples – being there to watch the temple cleansing and subsequent healings?

4. In the future, is there something you can do to stand up for the truth and what is right?

CHAPTER 4:

THE GRAND CONFRONTATION

After His triumphal entry, the cleansing of the temple, and the messianic proclamations, the tensions between Jesus and the Jewish leadership had reached a boiling point. It was apparent the chief priests, the Sadducees, and some of the Pharisees wanted Jesus gone. The straw that broke the proverbial camel's back was when they confronted Jesus in front of the Temple a day after the cleansing episode. Even though Jesus previously claimed to be the Messiah several times, He directed His comments this time to *the* highest-ranking Jewish leaders. He didn't mince words and instead sent a dagger through the heart of their hypocrisy.

His disciples had to sense things were at a tipping point, and Jesus was in grave danger. Of course, they wanted to protect Him, but the disciples still didn't understand the true purpose of His mission – to offer Himself up to die on the cross.

In high school, we used the phrases, "You burned him" or "You roasted him." Jesus was constantly roasting the Jewish leadership who tried to ensnare Him in their verbal traps – and this confrontation was no different. If I were Peter, James, or any of the other disciples, there are times when I would have thought: "Oh man, why do these guys keep coming back for more?" However, it's important to note that Jesus did what He did out of love. No matter the person, it was always a message of repentance and learning to honor the one true God.

I decided to include this event, what I call the "grand confrontation," because of the many lessons we can learn. To a degree, I expect that most of us have been hypocrites in one way or another, and Jesus' message during this confrontation also applies to us. I also included it because when the Sadducees, priests, scribes, and some of the Pharisees walked away from this, there was no doubt they wanted Jesus dead. As far as we know, nobody had previously called out their hypocrisy in such a direct, clear, and unmistakable way.

The Grand Confrontation

It was the day after He cleansed the temple. Jesus and His followers once again came up to the Temple with the intent to teach and heal. You can imagine that Jesus was a well-known figure in Jerusalem at this point. While walking on the temple grounds, the chief priests, scribes, and elders approached Him. Imagine being one of the disciples, standing next to Peter, when you see the group of Jewish leaders hastily crossing the courtyard with their robes billowing behind them. Picture yourself looking at Peter and thinking: "Here we go again. What are they going to do or say this time?"

When the leaders approached Jesus, He was likely already teaching and healing because they angrily asked Him: "By what authority doest thou these things? And who gave thee authority to do these things?" (Mark 11:28). Imagine standing next to Him and the intense atmosphere surrounding a confrontation like this!

Then, in His typical fashion, Jesus turned their own words on them and had them doing mental gymnastics to find an answer.

As noted in Mark 12:1, He "began to speak unto them by parables." Many other books go into each of the parables in detail. Rather than repeat what you can find in other places, I'll share a very brief summary of each. The focus is on imagining what it would have been like to be there witnessing this exchange and mentally being a part of that experience.

When I picture this great confrontation, I imagine Jesus' words and body language increasing in passion and intensity – to match the increasing intensity of the parables and woes. The focus of the parables started somewhat obscure, but by the end, there is no mistaking that Jesus was referencing them and their hypocrisy. Imagine seeing the reactions on the faces of the priests and scribes. I can picture the rage building in them, their faces turning red and even palpably shaking by the end. But truth cuts like a dagger, and they likely had no response because they *knew* what He said was true.

The Parable of the Two Sons (Matthew 21:28-32). Jesus stated that it would be easier for the repentant publicans and harlots to go into the kingdom of God than for the unrepentant rulers (the Jewish Leaders).

The Parable of the Wicked Husbandmen (Mark 12:1-11). The husbandmen (the Jewish leaders), watching over the vineyard, killed the heir and son of the vineyard owner.

After He related the first two parables, the priests and scribes were so enraged they "sought to lay hold on Him" (Mark 12:12). Imagine seeing the anger on their faces. Next, picture them aggressively moving towards Jesus to lay hold on him. But the people cried out in support of Jesus and raised their voices to protest the priests' aggression. Finally, visualize the priests looking around confused, realizing that the people sided with Jesus. The priests finally left, not knowing what else to do, and sent "certain Pharisees and Herodians to catch Him in His words" (Mark 12:13).

Once again, this new group of aggressors tried to trap Jesus by asking whether paying tribute to Caesar with Roman coinage was lawful. At that time, paying tribute to Caesar was heralding him as a god. Jesus answered: "Render unto Caesar that which is Caesar's, and to God the things that are God's" (Mark 12:17). Imagine the astonished look on their faces, realizing they couldn't trap Him.

Then He shared the following parable:

Parable of the Marriage of the King's Son (Matthew 22:2-10). The King prepared a great feast and sent his servants to call those who were invited, yet they wouldn't come. So the servants went to another place and called others who wanted to come (the house of Israel didn't answer the call, so the servants went to the Gentiles).

Then the Sadducees stepped forward from the crowd for their turn. They also attempted to trap Jesus by asking loaded questions about marriage and the resurrection. Once again, they were astonished by Jesus' answers. At this point, a large crowd had undoubtedly gathered. It appeared that those who left earlier had returned. So, imagine the scribes, Pharisees, priests, and Saddu-cees huddled together, dressed in their robes, squared up against Jesus. In contrast, picture Jesus dressed in a simple tunic, standing erect and confident, surrounded by His disciples and the favorable crowd. This thirty-three-year-old man stumped and silenced some of the most "learned" priests, scribes, Pharisees, and Hero-dians of the day with His responses and parables.

Finally, after multiple attempts to trap and snare Jesus, it was clear they weren't going to entangle Him in their web. Hence, from that point forward, "No man durst ask Him any question" (Mark 12:34). Therefore, Jesus turned the tables and began to teach and ask them questions.

He took on a direct tone with His words, and you can imag-ine the growing ire as the scribes and priests were powerless to do anything but listen. He started by expounding on the divine sonship of Christ and the example of the poor widow who gave everything she had. Then, He took a direct frontal assault on pride and hypocrisy and used them as an example.

The Woes

While referencing the leadership in front of Him, it's interesting that Jesus also spoke to the multitude and His disciples (Matthew 23:1). Imagine listening to these rebukes while watching the reac-tion of the temple priests and other leaders. Visualize Jesus turning to the crowd and making eye contact with the people, yet lifting His hand and gesturing towards the leadership while making these remarks:

- Beware of the scribes, which love to go in long clothing, and love salutations in the market (Mark 12:38).
- Whatsoever they bid you observe, that observe and do; but do not ye after their works: for they say, and do not (Matthew 23:3).
- But all their works they do to be seen of men (Matthew 23:5).
- Woe unto you, Scribes and Pharisees, hypocrites! For ye pay tithe of mint and anise and cumin, and have omitted the weightier matters of the law, judgment, mercy, and faith (Matthew 23:23).
- Woe unto you, Scribes and Pharisees, hypocrites! For ye are like unto whited sepulchers, which indeed appear beautiful outward, but are within full of dead men's bones, and of all uncleanness. Even so ye also outwardly appear righteous unto men, but within ye are full of hypocrisy and iniquity (Matthew 23:27 – 28).

Wow! What would you think and feel if you were in their shoes? He was right, and they knew it.

For years, the temple priests and leadership missed the whole point of the Gospel. They threw the adulterer at the feet of Jesus in condemnation, yet He showed compassion. They strained at Jesus healing a man on the Sabbath, but they missed the fact that He just healed a paralytic who hadn't walked in decades! With more than 613 laws, Jesus was calling out the blatant hypocrisy that was a deep part of the culture.

After this rebuke of hypocrisy, Jesus turned His back on the enraged priests and left the Temple. Although He would share some other parables with His disciples in private, these were the last public parables He would give before His crucifixion.

The temple priests and other leaders must have had the death sentence for Jesus already decreed in their minds. This confrontation was simply the "icing on the cake" to affirm their decree; they just had to work out the details on how to accomplish it. Imagine Peter, James, John, Lazarus, Mary, Martha, and the other disciples watching this unfold. They were intelligent people and had to realize what had happened in this grand confrontation. They already feared for His life; now, they must have been petrified after witnessing this direct callout of the Jewish leaders and seeing firsthand their anger.

His disciples were still in full "protection" mode. They didn't understand that Jesus was about to willingly offer Himself up in the great atoning sacrifice, which we'll discuss in the subsequent chapters.

Before concluding, however, there is a critical sidenote. Throughout the years, there have been many hate crimes against Jews for their history. This type of violence is the same kind of hypocrisy Jesus condemned during this confrontation. A genuine Christian should exemplify charity, mercy, and kindness to all people.

Reference Scriptures

Matthew 21:23 – 46

Matthew 22 & 23

Mark 11:28 – 33

Mark 12

Ponder, Visualize, and Personalize

Take a few minutes to visualize being there for the "grand confrontation." Imagine what it might have been like when He called
out pride and hypocrisy. Then, while you think about that and
the questions below, capture any thoughts or feelings in a journal.

1. Is there something in your life right now that might be
    considered hypocritical? In other words, are there places
    in your life where you are outwardly living the law, but
    inwardly it's a different story?

2. Evaluate your current perspective. Are there areas in your
    life where maybe you're straining over a gnat but missing
    the weightier matters of the Gospel? For example, are you
    so focused on a particular "program" or "doing something
    a certain way" that you're missing the bigger picture?

3. Are there times in your life when maybe you're more like
    the Jewish leadership than you might care to admit? If so,
    what are those places, and how can you change them?

PART TWO

THE LAST SUPPER TO THE RESURRECTION

CHAPTER 5:

THE LAST SUPPER

L ike so many events in Jesus' life, a person can quickly read about the facts of the Last Supper in a few verses, or it can become a sacred, revelatory experience if we imagine being there. When you mentally put yourself in the shoes of the disciples and visualize being there, the story comes to life and becomes very personal.

After the "grand confrontation" at the Temple, the day of Unleavened Bread was just around the corner – the day the Passover offering must be killed and eaten. So Jesus sent Peter and John to a follower's home to prepare a place where they could gather for this meal. He said to them, "Go into the city to a certain man [He obviously had someone specific in mind] and say unto him, the Master saith, my time is at hand; I will keep the Passover at thy house with my disciples" (Matthew 26:18).

What an honor it must have been for this man to be their host and have them as guests in the upper room of his house.

The gospel accounts vary in the order in which events took place that evening, so rather than worry about in what order they happened, we'll focus on the overall experience itself.

First, think about the setting in which they met. It was evening, and they gathered in the upper room of someone's home. The room likely would have had open windows with the typical shutters of the day. Imagine candles burning throughout the room to provide them with light. The temperature would have likely been around sixty to seventy degrees Fahrenheit in early April. In addition, you would be able to smell the aroma of the Passover meal. Picture the apostles seated around a table with Jesus seated in the middle (or wherever you picture Him seated).

When they sat to eat, Jesus proclaimed, "I have desired to eat this Passover with you before I suffer: For I say unto you, I will not any more eat thereof, until it be fulfilled which is written in the prophets concerning me" (Luke 22:15 – 16). This dinner would be His last meal in mortality.

Although the Apostles still couldn't predict the impending suffering that would later happen in Gethsemane or the looming crucifixion, they certainly had to sense this evening was serious. Things were changing; there was a lot of "finality" in Jesus' words that night. It was as if there was a passing of the torch taking place, yet they couldn't piece the puzzle together.

The seriousness also had to be weighing on Jesus as well. Everything He had prepared for since the premortal Grand Council in heaven was for this exact moment – what would happen in the next twenty-four hours.

The Betrayal

It's easy to gloss over the details but think about the impact on Jesus from the impending betrayal.

"He [Jesus] sat down with the twelve. And as they did eat, he said, verily I say unto you, that one of you shall betray me" (Matthew 26:21).

Imagine yourself sitting at the table when Jesus looked around, making eye contact with everyone, including you. Then, sadly, He states, "One of you will betray me." Yikes! I would feel terrified and devastated, and I would be begging that He wasn't referencing me. It appeared the apostles felt the same way. Picture the surprised looks of dismay on their faces when He suggested one of them would betray Him. They immediately felt the same worry I would feel and must have been looking at each other, wondering who it might be. Matthew described it well: "They were exceedingly sorrowful, and began every one of them to say unto him, Lord, is it I?" (Matthew 26:22).

Jesus, feeling the weight and sorrow of the betrayal, said, "Truly the Son of man goeth as it was determined: but woe unto that man by whom he is betrayed!" (Luke 22:22).

The Lord then lamented, "He it is, to whom I shall give a sop [morsel] when I have dipped it. When he had dipped the sop, he gave it to Judas. Then Judas, which betrayed him, answered and said, Master, is it I?" (John 13:26 – 27 and Matthew 26:23 – 26). Imagine Jesus' sorrowful response as He looked at Judas directly in the eyes – knowing He had already been sold for thirty pieces of silver – and said, "Thou has said. That thou doest, do quickly."

Judas got up and left with a dagger of truth shot through his heart. The disciples were confused and weren't sure what had happened. John described, "No man at the table knew for what intent he spake this unto him. Some of them thought because

Judas had the bag [took care of the money], that Jesus had said unto him, buy those things that we have need of against the feast; or, that he should give something to the poor" (John 13:28 – 29). None of the disciples could genuinely fathom that someone from their inner circle would betray Jesus, so the confusion becomes understandable.

Though we don't know all of the details about Judas, his intent, or his motivation, we know from the multiple gospels that the adversary, the Devil, deceived him, and he was the catalyst for Jesus' capture.

The Sacrament

As they were finishing the Passover meal, with Judas gone, the Lord was ready to introduce the sacrament of the "new covenant."

In Mark 14:20 – 26 (JST), he described the scene as follows:

As they did eat, Jesus took bread and blessed it, and brake, and gave to them, and said, take it, and eat.

Behold, this is for you to do in remembrance of my body; for as oft as ye do this ye will remember this hour that I was with you.

And he took the cup, and when he had given thanks, he gave it to them; and they all drank of it.

And he said unto them, This is in remembrance of my blood which is shed for many, and the new testament which I give unto you; for of me ye shall bear record unto all the world.

And as oft as ye do this ordinance, ye will remember me in this hour that I was with you and drank with you of this cup, even the last time in my ministry.

Verily I say unto you, Of this ye shall bear record; for I will no more drink of the fruit of the vine with you, until that day that I drink it new in the kingdom of God.

And now they were grieved, and wept over him.

Imagine if you were in the room hearing these words: "I will no more drink of the fruit of the vine with you" … "even the last time in my ministry" … "This in remembrance of my *blood* which is shed for many" … and "ye will remember me in this hour that I was with you." Wow! There's a lot of finality in those words.

Though still not completely clear, the puzzle was starting to come together in the disciples' minds that Jesus wouldn't be with them much longer. What sorrow they must have felt. Have you ever had to say goodbye to a loved one or a good friend? Furthermore, these disciples of three years gave up their professions, livelihood, and everything to follow Him. Try to feel what they must have felt and see if you can sense the solemnity of the moment. Imagine looking around the candle-lit room and seeing the tears streaking down the cheeks of Peter, John, and the other apostles as they try to process what they're hearing. As sad as they were, I doubt they realized they would be losing Jesus later that very night.

For us, the sacrament becomes authentic and memorable when we think of the rich symbolism. Sometimes when I take the sacrament today, I imagine Jesus being the one to administer it to me as the great High Priest. At the sacrament table today, the white veil resting over the table represents His body, the breaking of the bread represents His broken body, and the water or wine represents His blood that would be spilled multiple times in Gethsemane, with the lashings, and upon the cross.

It's an ordinance rich in symbolism, and the same promise and invitation offered that evening still applies to us today – remember Him!

The Washing of the Feet

A solemn mood permeated the room, but Jesus wasn't done instituting new ordinances or instructing His apostles.

After introducing the sacrament, Jesus stood up, grabbed a towel, and girded himself. He then poured water into a basin and "began to wash the disciples' feet, and to wipe them with the towel wherewith he was girded" (John 13:4 – 5).

This ritual (now becoming an ordinance) was a customary Jewish tradition, but Jesus was doing the work of the lowliest servants. The disciples must have been stunned by this act of humility and meekness – they should have been washing *His* feet, not the other way around.

How would you feel if you were in the room with them? It's one thing to read about, but imagine Jesus kneeling in front of you, gently picking up *your* feet to wash them, and looking into *your* eyes with a loving smile.

In that context, it's easy to understand Peter's response. When Jesus knelt in front of Peter, he exclaimed, "Thou needest not to wash my feet. Jesus answered him, If I wash thee not, thou hast no part with me. Simon Peter saith unto him, Lord, not my feet only, but also my hands and my head" (John 13:8 – 10).

As a side note, I've got to say I love Peter. I'm confident many of us would have felt like Peter in that situation. This is why Peter said something like, "No, don't wash my feet; I should be washing your feet." Jesus responded, "If I wash thee not, thou hast no part with me." Then, in his typical devoted and emotional response, Peter quickly said, "Lord, not my feet only, but also my hands and my head." I love imagining Peter saying, "Fine, if you need to wash my feet for me to be with you, then wash my whole body because I *always* want to be with you." Of course, I'm paraphrasing and putting some of my words in his mouth, but Peter's expressions make it easy to envision his thoughts and feelings at that moment.

After Jesus finished washing their feet, He sat back down and continued to teach them. "Ye call me Master and Lord: and ye say well; for so I am. If I then, your Lord and Master, have washed your feet; ye also ought to wash one another's feet. I have given you an example, that ye should do as I have done to you" (John 13: 12 – 16).

He's teaching a powerful leadership principle through servant leadership, a foreign principle in that era. Jesus demonstrated that the leader is also the servant and no better than the people they lead.

However, washing the feet was not just a humble act in itself or an example of servant leadership alone; it pointed to something new, something bigger – a new commandment. Before they finished eating, Jesus introduced one of His final and most profound teachings. "Little children [interesting He used that phrase], yet a little while I am with you. Ye shall seek me: and as I said unto the Jews, Whither I go, ye cannot come; so now I say to you. A new commandment I give unto you, that ye love one another; as I have loved you, that ye also love one another. By this shall all men know that ye are my disciples if ye have love one to another" (John 13:33 – 35).

From our current cultural perspective, the command to love one another makes perfect sense. However, this was revolutionary back then and bolstered everything Jesus taught up to that point (sermon on the mount, washing of the feet, etc.). Jesus reinforced that the whole essence of servant leadership is love! If there was any question about what that looked like, He clarified, *As I have loved you* (I washed your feet), love one another.

Despite this new teaching about love, what caught Peter's attention instead was, "whither I go, ye cannot come." So, Peter asked, "Lord, where are you going?" Jesus responded, "Whither I go, thou canst not follow me now; but thou shalt follow me afterwards." Again, in typical Peter fashion, he proclaimed, "Lord, why cannot I follow thee now? I will lay down my life for thy sake." Then, in another serious moment, Jesus responded – and it must have shocked Peter and the other disciples – "Wilt thou lay down thy life for my sake? Verily, I say unto thee, The cock shall not crow, til thou has denied me thrice" (John 13:35 – 38).

People often think of Jesus' response as foreshadowing Peter's denial later that night. However, I want to suggest a different perspective. Was that a foreshadowing statement to Peter, or was that a command? If it was a command, would that not have been one of the hardest things Peter would ever be asked to do – deny His Lord three times? But doing so would enable Peter to watch and witness Jesus' final hours at the hands of the priests and Romans. Peter, the devoted, loyal disciple, repeatedly showed no fear. He jumped off a boat and walked on water. He also stood next to Jesus to face the mob and smote the ear of a temple guard (that took guts), so why would he be afraid of a couple of random people asking if he associated with Jesus? When read in a command context, it changes the entire statement. Could you imagine how that must have hit Peter like a ton of bricks *if* that supposition is correct?

If that is correct, Peter must have thought, "Lord, how can you do this? How can you ask [command] me to deny thee three times before the night is out? What are you talking about?" The Bible gives us so few details that something like this perspective is worth considering. It would have changed the entire tenor of that conversation and would've been a true test of discipleship for Peter – he vowed to give his life; how could he be told to deny Jesus three times? It also sheds light on why he wept profusely when he denied him for the third time later that night.

Furthermore, *if* that supposition is correct, it also highlights a unique aspect of Jesus' love for His people. Jesus just finished giving the new commandment to love one another, and then he commanded Peter to do something that seemed odd and rather "unloving" – deny Him. This just shows that Jesus' perspective is beyond our minuscule understanding. When He commands, it's for our greater good and out of love.

The Wrap Up

It's easy to understand how emotionally exhausted the apostles would have been after this experience – just in time to walk to Gethsemane.

John tells us that after Jesus had spoken with His disciples throughout the meal, He offered up what I find to be one of the most intricate and meaningful prayers ever captured. It's worth reading carefully to see how it applies to us (John 17). After this powerful prayer, and before leaving for Gethsemane, they sang a hymn together. I love singing hymns because it invites a strong spirit, and I often feel upbeat and inspired. However, I'm not sure this was one of those times. It would have been difficult to focus on a hymn after these incredible proclamations and experiences. Most of them were probably singing while thinking, "So, what's going to happen next?"

The evening was monumental, and the apostles' heads must have been swirling, trying to process everything Jesus had done and taught them. Think about all that happened: Judas left, they ate the Passover meal, Jesus instituted the sacrament, washed their feet, taught them about servant leadership, and finally, concluded the evening with a beautiful prayer and singing a hymn. Jesus knew what lay ahead of Him at this point, but the apostles didn't. He was focused, ready, and anxious to get to it, but they were exhausted and perplexed and had no idea that the evening was just getting started!

Reference Scriptures

John 13

D&C 88:139 – 141

Matthew 26:17 – 30

Mark 14:12 – 31

Luke 22:7 – 38

Ponder, Visualize, and Personalize

Take a few minutes to visualize being there for the Last Supper. Then, while you think about that and the questions below, capture any thoughts or feelings in a journal.

1. What would you feel if you watched Jesus kneel in front of *you* to wash *your* feet?

2. Have you ever been asked by the Lord to do something difficult? What was the result of acting on it?

3. How can we treat the sacrament as a holy and sacred experience?

4. While you ponder His final commandment, how can you more fully love and serve others?

5. Do you remember when you allowed somebody else to serve you? How did you feel?

CHAPTER 6:

GETHSEMANE

This seems like an appropriate place in the book to pause. What is about to unfold in this chapter, and the remainder of the book, became the most pivotal events in human history.

Eons before that evening, Jesus stepped forward in the Grand Councils of heaven to say, "Here am I, send me."

Adam and Eve knew they would be redeemed from their transgression because of what Jesus would do in the next twenty-four hours. Likewise, the many people who lived the law of sacrifice (sacrificing the unblemished lamb) for thousands of years prior did so because it pointed toward this moment. The law of Moses was given to Israel to orient them towards Christ and the events that were about to unfold right now.

In the Church of Jesus Christ, we believe that we are all spiritual children of Heavenly Parents and lived as spirits, without a body, in a pre-mortal existence, before coming to earth. With that context, imagine what we were doing while Christ entered the garden of Gethsemane that evening. Imagine, as heavenly spirits, looking in on the scene as He was subsequently tried and crucified, and when He ultimately became the first fruits of the resurrection. God the Father, Adam, Eve, Moses, Abraham, and every one of us, along with millions of others, watched with eager anticipation. What would that have looked like from heaven, knowing everything we had supported for eons was about to happen?

Jesus, the firstborn and only begotten son of God the Father in the flesh, was about to step forward and fulfill the grand assignment He willingly volunteered to fulfill. It was this assignment on which hung all of God's plan.

Jesus is willing to personally reveal the events that transpired that night (and the subsequent days) to those who make an effort to ponder, pray, and search. He has a pattern of doing so through history, and this type of personal revelation is for those who genuinely seek Him regardless of calling, race, gender, or background. However, we can't rush revelation and make it happen on our timeline. Instead, He will reveal these things to us individually in His own time, in His own way, and according to His will (D&C 88:67-68).

The Stage is Set

After the emotionally taxing Passover dinner, Jesus and the twelve "went out into the mount of Olives...unto a place called Gethsemane" (Matthew 26:30 & 36).

Let's learn a little more about the garden of Gethsemane to visualize better what it was like to be there.

It was a familiar place to the disciples and Jesus, who frequented Gethsemane numerous times to visit and teach. The garden is near the eastern entrance to Jerusalem (the Golden Gate). Leaving Jerusalem, you would descend a small hill into the Kidron Valley before climbing the Mount of Olives. As you ascend out of the Kidron Valley, you will find Gethsemane at the base of the western slope of the Mount of Olives. It's a relatively small area, and, as the name describes, it's filled with ancient olive trees that are at least 1,000 years old.

In Jesus' time, the highway that left Jerusalem and climbed the Mount of Olives passed near the garden. Hence, it would have been easy to see any group or procession of people leaving Jerusalem at night, especially if they were carrying torches.

It's also interesting to note that Gethsemane means "oil press" in Hebrew. The extraction process for olives requires extreme pressure to get even a tiny amount of oil. As one of many symbols that night, Jesus would experience more pressure and pain than any mortal had ever experienced.

The Entrance

Imagine joining Jesus and His apostles as they walked from inside the Jerusalem gates to Gethsemane, which would have taken them about twenty to thirty minutes. The temperature would have dropped slightly to create a chill in the air. It would have been dark except for the light of the stars and the torches they were carrying.

Would they have walked in silence, contemplating what had already happened that evening? Or were they talking about why they were walking out to the garden at such a late hour?

Mark notes that when they arrived at the garden, "The disciples began to be sore amazed, and to be very heavy, and to complain in their hearts, wondering if this be the Messiah" (JST Mark 14:36).

Have you ever been in a place that felt "heavy" or the "mood" palpable? Imagine being with them when they arrived in the garden feeling this oppressive sense of sorrow and heaviness. Picture looking at the solemn faces of the apostles, each trying to navigate their respective thoughts and feelings about what was happening.

Some of the disciples may have wondered if He was truly the Messiah because of all the finality they had just experienced at the Last Supper. Still not fully understanding His purpose, some may have questioned, "I thought the Messiah was supposed to claim His kingship and overthrow the Romans." Instead, it's becoming more apparent that He will leave them, shattering their expectations of freedom from Roman oppression. It might be easy to be critical of them, but that's coming from our current perspective and knowing how these events played out. Plus, if they were like most people, no one is at their best when exhausted, and this had already been a long day for them. Therefore, it's no wonder the scriptures tell us that in their hearts, some questioned *if* He indeed was the Messiah.

Knowing their hearts, Jesus said to them, "Sit ye here, while I shall pray. Then, he taketh Peter, James, and John, and rebuked them, and said unto them, My soul is exceeding sorrowful, even unto death; tarry ye here and watch [stay awake]" (Mark 14:32 – 33).

When Jesus says, "My soul is exceeding sorrowful," that should grab our attention. Imagine watching Him walk deeper into the garden and seeing the focus, determination, and solemnity on His face as the weight of the looming task settled over Him.

While the scriptures don't elaborate on many details, it seemed like the Savior was saying to His most trusted group of three, "it doesn't matter if you're tired; I need *your* support. You should know better than to murmur in your hearts. Stay awake and watch what's about to happen."

The Suffering and Atonement

If you were writing this book, how would you put into words something so intense, personal, and sacred as what happened next? It's somewhat of a daunting task to expound on, and it's something so intimate and touching; hence, why I invite you to visualize being there and make it *your* experience with the Lord.

Imagine sitting by Peter, James, and John, watching Jesus walk a stone's throw away and kneel. At some point, they dozed off, but if they had stayed awake, they would have visibly seen Jesus' physical pain increasing.

In that tumultuous and redeeming evening, Jesus experienced numerous waves of increasing pain and suffering. These waves of suffering swept over Him physically, mentally, emotionally, and spiritually.

King Benjamin saw the events from that evening more than one hundred years before it happened and described them by saying, "He shall suffer temptations, and pain of body, hunger, thirst, and fatigue, *even more than man can suffer, except it be unto death*; for behold, *blood cometh from every pore, so great shall be his anguish for the wickedness and the abominations of his people*" (Mosiah 3:7, emphasis mine).

In many ways that none of us can fathom, He experienced the evilest, most vile, and wicked things any human could inflict upon another. He experienced it both from the perspective of the perpetrator and the victim. He knew and experienced the horror and regret of wicked men when they see the truth. He knew what Annas and Caiaphas, the two High Priests who later condemned Him, would feel upon realizing what they had done or how the Roman soldiers who would later flog and crucify Him would feel when they understood who He was.

He also experienced firsthand the excruciating emotional and physical pain suffered by the victims. He felt everything a person who was offended or violated would feel. He understood the natural resentment and anger a victim would often experience after being hurt or violated.

He learned what it felt like to lose a loved one, be diagnosed with a disease, lose hope, feel depressed and alone, and every other anguish and heartache imaginable.

Through hope, charity, and the love of God the Father, Jesus had to navigate how to overcome the evil and hopeless feelings associated with these events. Amongst it all, He learned to come to peace and find reconciliation with the Father.

These waves of torment and pain increased so much that even He was surprised by the intensity. Finally, so intense became the assault that "He fell on his face, and prayed, saying, O my Father, if it be possible, let this cup pass from me: nevertheless not as I will, but as thou wilt" (Matthew 26:39).

How do we put into words this sacred experience?

As painful as it is to imagine, picture the Savior sprawled on the ground face first, groaning and writhing in anguish, crying out to His Father. Imagine what the Father must have felt watching His perfect Son cry out in pain, knowing He can't intervene or stop it because there was no other way.

Matthew said, "There appeared an angel unto him from heaven, *strengthening* him." Though we can only speculate what was said, imagine the encouragement and the support this unnamed angel offered. Although I hesitate to attempt it, maybe the angel said something like, "You are the only one who can redeem the Father's creations from the fall. You are the only one who can do this. If you don't, all men will be lost. The hosts of heavens are cheering for you; we're all here with you. We love you! You can do this!"

Then, picture the resurgence in confidence as Luke described the Lord using every ounce of strength, "Being in agony he prayed *more earnestly*: and his sweat was as it were great drops of blood falling down to the ground" (Luke 22:44, emphasis mine).

This final wave of anguish and suffering became so intense He was physically wounded.

Several years ago, I visited Gethsemane. Of course, we don't know the *exact* spot where Jesus prayed, but simply being there in the garden was a beautiful experience. Not many people were visiting that day, so I went to a corner of the garden and prayed by myself – imagining what it would have been like to be present that night and thanking Him for all He did. A tender, beautiful, and personal moment occurred as I felt the Spirit of the Lord descend upon me. I felt the warmth and fire in my chest, testifying to the reality of Jesus and what happened in that sacred spot. I looked at the surrounding olive trees, each standing about twenty feet in the air, and wondered what it would have been like to sit amongst those trees and witness one of the greatest triumphs ever.

Some doubt whether or not He really bled from every pore, but Jesus confirmed the intense pain centuries later, "Which suffering caused myself, even God, the greatest of all, to tremble because of pain, and to bleed at every pore, and to suffer both body and spirit – and would that I might not drink the bitter cup, and shrink – Nevertheless, glory be to the Father, and I partook and finished my preparations unto the children of men" (D&C 19:18 – 19).

Finally, it was finished – He did it. He partook of the bitter cup that was His to drink. He suffered and overcame every imaginable wrong a human could experience. He experienced every pain, hurt, sorrow, and loss conceivable. He descended below all things so that He could rise above all things. Thus was Alma's prophecy fulfilled, which said, "He will take upon him their infirmities, that his bowels may be filled with mercy, according to the flesh, that he may know according to the flesh how to succor his people according to their infirmities" (Alma 7:12).

As a side note, I flew F-16 fighter jets for several years. When modern, high-speed aircraft like these turn, the centrifugal force or strain (called G's) on the pilot's body increases dramatically. When we would pull 9 G's (equivalent to about 1,800 pounds of force on the body) during a flight, we often returned with "geezles" – tiny red dots all over our shoulders, chest, or back. Geezles show up when capillaries burst under the strain of high G forces. That's at 9 G's – what type of incredibly intense pressure would it take to cause a person to bleed from every pore? While it's not even comparable, He must have been pressed beyond anything humanly imaginable if He bled from every pore.

Now that His Atonement in Gethsemane was finished and He experienced every pain, infirmity, or emotion a person could experience, how did He feel when He stood up?

Imagine seeing Him stand up and walk towards His three apostles, exhausted, with blood all over His body. In addition, His tunic would have been red with the blood that soaked through it. His disciples were physically and emotionally exhausted, so much so they couldn't keep their eyes open despite their best efforts. When Jesus approached the sleeping apostles, visualize Him saying with a mix of resignation, determination, and love, "Sleep on now, and take your rest: behold, the hour is at hand, and the Son of Man is betrayed into the hands of sinners" (Mark 14:41).

Picture the surprised faces of Peter, James, and John when they woke to see Jesus through the faint torchlight, covered in blood and likely pale because of the dramatic experience. Then, imagine the feelings they must have felt to realize they fell asleep *again*, only to hear Him say, "the Son of Man is betrayed into the hands of sinners."

Despite everything He had experienced, Jesus knew there was still more to do. Though His purpose in Gethsemane was finished, His overall mission wasn't. Like His disciples, He had to be exhausted after Gethsemane, yet some of the most challenging physical tests were still ahead, and He knew it. Again, I'm in awe of Jesus.

Once again, the scriptures only give us vague details. For example, did Jesus change His tunic? Did one of His disciples give his tunic to Jesus to replace His stained one? Did Jesus take a few minutes to wash off the dried blood in a nearby stream?

Whatever happened between Jesus waking His apostles and His betrayal will remain a mystery unless it is revealed to us personally.

After He roused the apostles, imagine looking across the Kidron Valley and seeing a procession of people leaving Jerusalem with torches burning. Can you picture this mob descending the hill from Jerusalem, crossing the Kidron Valley, and ascending towards the garden? From the time they left Jerusalem's gate, it would only be a few minutes until they arrived at the garden. Hence, why Jesus said, "Rise up, let us go; he that betrayeth me is at hand" (Mark 14:42).

The Betrayal and Capture

After Jesus woke His apostles, the scriptures tell us that Judas arrived, and "with him a great multitude with swords and staves" and lanterns and torches (John 18:3). Among this multitude included "the Chief Priests and the scribes and elders" (Mark 14:43).

Imagine Jesus walking out from the inner garden to meet the approaching mob. When the mob reached the garden and saw Jesus, picture the look on their faces. The men in the mob must have been anxious, looking around nervously, wondering if an ambush or trap might be awaiting them. But, on the other hand, imagine Jesus standing there with confidence and poise – in total control.

Jesus questioned the approaching mob, "Whom seek ye?" They answered, "Jesus of Nazareth." Imagine hearing His majestic response, "I am he." Immediately the mob "went backward and fell to the ground" (John 18:4-6). John is the only one who mentions this, so something about the power in Jesus' voice and

His majesty must have caused them all to step back, realizing His power was beyond what they understood.

During this initial exchange, Judas stepped forward and gave the signaled kiss he had pre-arranged with the mob's leaders to identify Jesus. "He came to Jesus, and said, hail, master; and kissed him." Think of the heartbreak Jesus must have felt at this ultimate betrayal with a kiss. As Judas pulled away, imagine Jesus holding him by the shoulders, looking directly into his eyes, and saying to him with sorrow and sadness in His voice, "Friend [such a powerful term considering the circumstances], wherefore art thou come?" (Matthew 26:49-50). In other words, Jesus was saying, "Judas, why are you here with this group? Why did you do this?" How could anyone escape those soul-searching eyes? Therefore, imagine the look in Judas' eyes when he realized what he'd done, and the reality settled in his soul that he had just betrayed the Son of Man.

At Judas' signal, the mob rushed forward and "laid their hands on Jesus." Peter, the devoted disciple, "Drew his sword, and smote off his [Malchus, the servant of the High Priest] ear." Imagine Jesus stretching His hand towards Peter and lovingly rebuking him by saying, "Put up again thy sword. Thinkest thou that I cannot now pray to my Father, and he shall presently give me more than twelve legions of angels? But how then shall the scriptures be fulfilled, that thus it may be?" (Matthew 26:51 – 54).

Despite all the commotion and intensity of the moment, Jesus reached out and calmly touched Malchus' ear and healed him instantly. Can you picture the surprised look on Malchus' face when he realized their soon-to-be prisoner had just healed him?

I envision a total look of confusion as he immediately reassessed everything he thought he knew.

Jesus, in one final rebuke of the mob, said, "Are ye come out as against a thief with swords and staves to take me? I sat daily with you teaching in the Temple, and ye laid no hold on me" (Matthew 26:55).

At that point, Jesus allowed the mob to take Him. Bound at the wrists, they led Him away to one of the world's most illegal, corrupt tribunals.

Most of the disciples fled, but Peter followed the mob from afar off, even into the High Priest's palace.

Thus concluded one of the most sacred, intense, and holy experiences ever witnessed by man. But it was not over for Jesus; this was just the start of a sleepless journey through the trials, lashing, and ultimately to the cross.

Reference Scriptures

Mathew 26: 36 – 56

Mark 14:32 – 50

Luke 22:39 – 54

John 18:1 – 13

D&C 19:15 – 19

Prophetic References

Isaiah 53:6

Isaiah 53:11

Zechariah 13:7

2 Nephi 9:7

Mosiah 3:7

Mosiah 14:10

Alma 7:11 – 14

Helaman 5:9

Ponder, Visualize, and Personalize

Take a few minutes to visualize being in the garden on that great and terrible night. Then, while you think about it and answer the questions below, capture any thoughts or feelings in a journal.

1. What does Gethsemane and the Atonement mean to you?

2. Jesus commands us to repent because He already suffered, and we don't need to carry those burdens. Is there something you can repent of, or give to Him, so you don't carry that load anymore?

3. How do you show your gratitude to Jesus and our Heavenly Father?

4. If the Lord were to show you this scene and allow you to witness it, how would you feel?

CHAPTER 7:

THE TRIAL AND ROMAN LASHINGS

Jesus bled and suffered beyond anything we can imagine. A kiss from Judas betrayed him, and most of His disciples fled. Only two remained, Peter and John, and they followed Him from a distance. On that dark and chilly night, the mob led Him like a lamb to the slaughter as they walked towards Jerusalem. Although He was exhausted, I'm confident that if we walked with the mob, we would see a committed, focused look in Jesus' eyes as they reflected in the torchlight.

When they reached Jerusalem, the tribunals began. Although the various accounts of the trial highlight different details, they all agree on the overall structure, injustice, and evil by which the trials were conducted to arrive at the pre-determined guilty verdict.

John notes that the guards first took Jesus to the de facto leader, Annas, for an informal inquiry. Annas, the previous Chief Priest and the father-in-law to Caiaphas (the current Chief Priest) was a wicked man who wielded enormous power from his wealthy position of influence. If one looks into Jewish history, it's clear that if Annas wanted something done, the Sanhedrin and many of his family members would do whatever was needed to make it happen.

After a short visit, Annas sent Jesus to "Caiaphas the high priest, where the scribes and the elders were assembled" (John 14:13 and Matthew 26:57). There was no question Annas was behind the scenes directing the Sanhedrin to find a way to kill Jesus who, as you remember from Chapter 3, disrupted their money-making machine in the Temple and threatened their way of life.

They finally had their man, and the stage was set for one of the world's most corrupt, evil, and darkest trials.

The Sanhedrin

Interestingly, the Sanhedrin violated their own rules and laws to arrange the death of Jesus. For example, there were to be no trials after dark. They should have held the trial during daylight hours and in a public venue. Furthermore, it was Passover, and no trial should ever have happened on a feast day. In capital punishment cases, they could issue a verdict on the same day but must wait until the following day to find him liable (which is why they should never have met that night).

Also, to have a council, there had to be at least twenty-three members of the Sanhedrin – consisting of Sadducees, Pharisees, elders, and scribes. Though we don't know exactly who was present for the trial that night, we know there were at least twenty-three people because it was considered a council.

Imagine Jesus, most likely past midnight now, standing in an ornate and well-decorated hall (Caiaphas' palace), wearing a simple tunic with his hands bound. You would likely have seen numerous torches burning throughout the hall. The tension in the hall must have been palpable.

Have you ever been in a group where you were the minority, and everyone around you was vehemently and openly opposed to your views? If so, maybe you felt the group's disdain and maybe even open hostility. Think about Jesus standing in that tense environment, among the crowd of priestly leaders dressed in their religious attire, with malice and hatred in their eyes. Imagine being in the room hearing all the side conversations about this "Jesus of Nazareth" who finally stood before them on their terms.

At that point, the rigged trial began: "The chief priests and all the council *sought* for false witness against Jesus to put him to death; and found none" (Mark 14:55). There was nothing fair about this trial. It was wickedly biased from the beginning with only one acceptable outcome, so they *sought false* accusers. In other words, they looked for people willing to lie and say whatever was necessary to convict Jesus. These were pre-arranged witnesses, yet, "Many bare false witness against him, but their witness agreed not together" (Mark 14:56).

In any other setting, the inconsistency in the witnesses might have been comical or even embarrassing. Here were the most educated men in Jerusalem, and it must have been evident to everyone what a joke this was – they were grasping at straws. The witnesses couldn't even get the details of their own stories right, let alone get them to match.

Imagine seeing the frustrated and exasperated looks on the faces of the priests after each witness messed up their story. Picture Jesus standing there, resolute, in silence, watching witness after witness trip over themselves.

Finally, this debacle was embarrassing enough that Caiaphas decided to take matters into his own hands. Caiaphas "arose, and said unto him, Answerest thou nothing? What is it which these witness against thee? But Jesus held his peace" (Matthew 26:62 – 63). Imagine seeing this intense face-off between the Chief Priest and the true High Priest, one dressed in royal garb and the other in a simple tunic. One angry and ruffled, the other calm and majestic. Imagine Jesus looking directly into Caiaphas' eyes, not saying a word but holding His peace.

Then Caiaphas, even more angry, said, "I adjure thee by the living God, that thou tell us whether thou be the Christ, the Son of God."

Jesus responded with power and confidence, "I am. And ye shall see the Son of man sitting on the right hand of power; coming in the clouds of heaven" (Mark 14:62). Imagine the audible gasps that would have reverberated through the room and the astounded looks that must have passed between the council members. At that powerful declaration, Caiaphas rent his clothes and shouted, "what need we of any further witnesses? Ye have heard blasphemy: what think ye? And they all condemned him to be guilty of death" (Mark 14:63 – 65). They found their "reason" to sentence Him to death. Ironically, it was only blaspheming if He wasn't who He was.

The conviction wasn't enough for some of the people in the room. There were likely some present whom Jesus previously had embarrassed in the Temple or at the "grand confrontation" earlier that week. They were still seething with anger. So, not missing the opportunity, they "Began to spit on him, cover his face, buffet him, and say to him, Prophesy: and the servants did strike him with the palms of their hands" (Mark 14:65).

Neil A. Maxwell gave one of the best definitions of meekness I've ever heard: "To be poised under provocation." Imagine seeing Jesus, the Redeemer, standing like a lamb in a den of ravaging lions. Picture person after person walking up to Him, spitting in his face, backhanding Him, and mocking Him. Imagine Jesus, with red cheeks and moist eyes from being slapped, spittle oozing down his cheeks, not engaging or responding – poised under provocation, a perfect example of meekness. Once again, I'm in total awe of His control.

That night the wicked Sanhedrin accomplished their objective – they issued a death sentence on Jesus.

We don't know what they did with Jesus for the short time between the end of the trial and the sunrise. But, when the morning came, "they took counsel against Jesus to put him to death" (Matthew 27:1). In other words, they made sure they had their story straight because they would have to convince the Roman authorities to carry out the unjust sentence they couldn't legally execute.

The Roman Trial

The Sanhedrin delivered Jesus to Pontius Pilate – the Roman governor – to ratify their death sentence on Friday morning.

I'm not sure how you feel after pulling an all-nighter, but in the extremely rare instance when that happens, I'm completely exhausted and feel like I'm running on fumes. So, likewise, after Gethsemane and being up all night, Jesus had to be mentally, emotionally, and physically drained.

Yet, here He stood amidst the Romans, face-to-face with Pilate. A multitude of the Sanhedrin still surrounded them. Knowing blasphemy meant nothing to Rome, the priests and elders accused Jesus, saying, "We found this fellow perverting the nation, and forbidding to give tribute to Caesar, saying he himself is Christ a King" (Luke 23:2). Once again, they said whatever was necessary to provoke enough Roman ire to warrant the death penalty through fraud and deception – they were accusing Him of treason (totally different than their previous accusation of blasphemy).

Hearing the accusations from the Jewish leaders, Pilate asked Jesus, "Art thou the King of the Jews?" Jesus responded, "I am, even as thou sayest" (Mark 15:2).

Once again, this statement fired up the priests and elders. They angrily "accused him of many things: but he answered nothing" (Mark 15:3). Imagine being there in the assembly hall witnessing this exchange. Pilate is standing in front of Jesus with a curious look, surrounded by the religious leaders dressed in their shawls and priestly robes. Like the prior evening, the priests had to be incensed with anger at the messianic answer from Jesus that He was the King of the Jews. Imagine the priests getting right up in His face, pointing their fingers, and railing against Him with all kinds of accusations. Yet, just like the night prior, He stood calm, confident, and majestic, looking straight ahead.

Most people would have been nervous, emotional, or lost their composure to defend themselves – but not Jesus. Instead, He stood there with perfect poise and calm. So much so that Pilate asked Him, "Answerest thou nothing? Behold, how many things they witness against thee" (Mark 15:4). This time, Jesus chose not to answer Him either and stood there focused and unwavering.

Pilate had never seen so much poise, discipline, and control in his life, so much so that "he marveled" (Mark 15:4 – 5).

But, there was more to the story. Pilate's wife warned, "Have nothing to do with that just man: for I have suffered many things this day in a dream because of him" (Matthew 27:19). Though Pilate was a ruthless governor and issued the death penalty to countless people, his wife's dream combined with this incredible encounter made him nervous, wondering who this man really was.

Pilate looked at the priests and said, "I find no fault in this man."

Seeing their conviction slipping, the priests grew fiercer and accused Jesus of stirring up the people in Galilee. Because there were so many zealots in Galilee, they were trying to hit another sore spot for the Romans. When Pilate discovered Jesus was from Galilee, it gave him the out he was looking for. Pilate decided to send Jesus to Herod because Galilee was under his jurisdiction. Pilate thought, "Good, let Herod deal with this; I don't want anything more to do with Jesus."

So, Pilate sent Jesus to Herod, who anxiously sought an opportunity to meet with this man whose fame had spread throughout the region (not to mention Herod killed Jesus' cousin John). But, it was a short-lived and anti-climactic visit because although Herod questioned Him, Jesus chose to remain silent and did not answer any of his questions. Therefore, seeing nothing was coming from this visit, Herod returned Him to Pilate.

Pilate, upon receiving Jesus again, "Called together the *chief priests* and the *rulers* and the *people,* and said unto them, Ye have brought this man unto me, as one that perverteth the people: and, behold, I, having examined him before you, have found no fault in this man touching those things whereof ye accuse him: No, nor Herod. I will therefore chastise him and release him" (Luke 23:13 – 15 emphasis mine).

According to John, Pilate thought if he scourged and whipped Jesus, that would be enough to satisfy the people. Therefore, he sent Jesus to the Praetorium to be scourged and to appease the mob.

The Roman Lashings

The Roman lashings are almost as brutal to imagine as Gethsemane.

Each of the gospels put the lashings at a slightly different time in the trial process. For example, Matthew and Mark indicate that Jesus was first convicted by the mob and then scourged just before carrying the cross to Calvary. John's timing makes more sense – that the Romans first scourged Him to appease the Jewish mob. John suggests that Pilate attempted to hurt Him enough to satisfy the people without killing Him.

Regardless of the exact timing or motive, let's focus on the experience and how amazing it was that Jesus condescended to go through this.

The Romans led Jesus to the assembly hall, or Praetorium, "and gathered unto him the whole band of soldiers" (Matthew 27:27). Other translations say, "a whole cohort was gathered." A cohort is a tenth of the Legion, which means they gathered five-hundred soldiers. Clearly, the tension was palpable, and this was a high-stakes affair. Pilate didn't want any mistakes, riots, or missteps.

The Romans were very good at what they did when it came to scourging and inflicting pain. They had multiple balls and shards on the whip, designed to bruise and tear the skin. The whip was called a flagrum and was explicitly designed to maximize pain. Jesus was likely whipped thirty-nine times – the maximum number of lashings allowed by the Romans (2 Corinthians 11:24).

Imagine watching Jesus being led into the hall and bound to a solitary pole in the middle of the courtyard. Next, picture the band of Roman soldiers lining the courtyard walls with their armor, swords, and red linen undergarments. Finally, imagine a muscular executioner (the one responsible for the scourging) approaching Jesus while the other guard tightened His hands on the pole so He couldn't move.

As difficult as it is to visualize, picture the executioner winding up, and with as much strength as he can muster, swinging the whip forward and lashing Jesus' back. Imagine the excruciating look of pain and the audible gasp when He felt the first impact of the whip that both bruised and tore His skin. Can you imagine this scene repeating itself another thirty-eight times?

I estimate that it took approximately twenty to thirty seconds per lash, including the recovery time between lashes. Therefore, the entire lashing likely took approximately ten to fifteen minutes. That must have felt like an eternity for Jesus.

For many people, the lashings were enough to kill them. Take a second to imagine the pain you would feel on your own back after just *one* lash!

This scourging is another experience, like Gethsemane, where I can envision God having to turn away His face because of how difficult this must have been to watch. Here was His perfect Son being whipped, tortured, and mocked by the hardened Roman soldiers, and yet, to fulfill the plan, He couldn't intervene.

Imagine the soldier untying Jesus' hands from the pole and Jesus collapsing to the ground, lacking the strength to stand – especially after thirty-nine lashings. Then, as if it weren't enough, imagine the soldiers forcing Him up to His knees with blood dripping on the ground. Finally, envision one of the soldiers placing a crown of thorns on His head and pushing it down into His skin, causing new streaks of blood to flow down His face. Then, according to Matthew, "They put a reed in his right hand, and they bowed the knee before him and mocked him" (Matthew 27:29). John descriptively added, "the soldiers plaited a crown of thorns, and put it on his head, and they put on him a purple robe, and said, *Hail, King of the Jews*! And they smote him with their hands" (John 19:2 – 3).

Can you picture Jesus on His knees trembling because of pain, with a purple robe wrapped around Him, a crown of thorns on His head, covered with blood, and a reed in His hand?

Imagine the soldiers, dressed in armor, kneeling next to Him with their hands cupped together in mock adoration. Then, envision them looking at each other and laughingly shouting, "Hail, King of the Jews!"

I can hardly imagine the moment when those soldiers learned later who it was who kneeled in front of them. Little did they know that they were contributing to a powerfully symbolic moment. The crown of thorns upon Jesus' head symbolized His kingship, a purple robe and reed in hand symbolized His royalty, and mocking Him while on their knees symbolized hailing Him as the King. If only they knew they were mocking the true King and creator of the world.

Someday, those same people will bow their knees again in front of Him, not to mock, but in kneeling adoration. It will be a humble acknowledgment of Him as their real King.

The Final Sentence

After the lashing and mockery, Pilate brought Jesus back to the courtyard, where the people were gathered. It's important to note that the Sanhedrin had organized and rallied up the crowd to do their bidding for them. This gathering was more of a mob than a true representation of the people of Jerusalem — many of whom considered Jesus to be the Messiah.

With Jesus standing nearby wearing the purple robe and the crown of thorns, Pilate exclaimed, "I bring him forth to you, that ye may know that I find no fault in him." Then, Pilate shouted to the people, "Behold, the man!" (John 19:4 – 5).

Yet, the priests cried to the mob, "Crucify him, crucify him" (John 19:6). It was customary for the Roman authorities to release a Jewish prisoner at Passover. Pilate asked whether they should release Jesus or Barabbas, who was in jail for theft at the time. Matthew notes that "the chief priests and elders *persuaded* the multitude that they should ask for Barabbas, and destroy Jesus" (Matthew 27:20, emphasis mine). Pilate tried to offer an exchange, but the mob wanted none of it, and Pilate released Barabbas instead. Once again, Jesus stood alone, bloodied, yet resolute.

Imagine the priests and elders looking at the surrounding crowd encouraging them by yelling, "crucify him," and inciting the mob to join in their chants. At this point, the possessed Jewish leaders wanted blood, which was the only thing that would satisfy their arrogant lust.

Pilate asked a final time, "What shall I do then with Jesus, which is called the Christ?" The crowd cried out and yelled, "Let him be crucified!" (Matthew 27:22).

Therefore, "When Pilate saw he could prevail nothing, but rather a tumult was made, he took water and washed his hands before the multitude. Then delivered he him therefore unto them to be crucified" (Matthew 27:24).

Imagine being in the crowd and hearing the chants and wicked calls of the people. Then, picture Pilate standing on a rise, washing his hands in a basin (as if that would liberate him from the consequences of his decision), and signaling his guards to deliver Jesus to the mob.

Thus, the words Jesus spoke earlier to His apostles were so far fulfilled, "We go up to Jerusalem, and all things that are written by the prophets concerning the Son of man shall be accomplished. For he shall be delivered to the Gentiles, and shall be mocked, and spitefully entreated, and spit upon. And they shall scourge him and put him to death" (Luke 18:31 – 34).

Nephi's eloquent and prophetic words were also fulfilled: "And the world, because of their iniquity, shall judge him to be a thing of naught; wherefore they scourge him, and he suffereth it; and they smite him, and he suffereth it. Yea, they spit upon him, and he suffereth it, because of his loving kindness and his long-suffering towards the children of men" (1 Nephi 19:9).

Jesus could have stopped this evil conviction and trial at any time. Yet, He remained poised under provocation and focused on fulfilling the mission that only He could fulfill on behalf of the entire human race.

Beginning at the arrest in Gethsemane to the final Roman conviction by Pilate, this was the culmination of one of the craziest facades and unfair trials in history. The entire thing was a setup inspired by Lucifer and carried out by his followers in the name of religion. Many people in Jerusalem recognized Jesus as the Messiah, but the loud voice of the Sanhedrin trumped the people's wishes, and they got what they had planned for months – the death of Jesus.

Reference Scriptures

Mathew 26:57 – 67; 27:1 – 31

Mark 14:55 – 65; 15:1 - 20

Luke 23:1 – 25

John 18:19 – 40; 19:1 – 16

Prophetic References

Isaiah 53:3 – 11

Luke 18:31 – 34

Zechariah 13:7

Mark 10:33 – 34

1 Nephi 19:9, 13

2 Nephi 9:7

Mosiah 3:9

Mosiah 14:2 – 5

Mosiah 15:5 – 7

Alma 7:11 – 13

Helaman 5:9

Ponder, Visualize, and Personalize

Take a few minutes to visualize being there for these unfair trials and the Roman lashings. Then, while you think about that and the questions below, capture any thoughts or feelings in a journal.

1. How would you feel if you were in the Sanhedrin to watch the trial or in the courtyard to see the lashings?

2. What is one way you can express your gratitude to the Lord for all He did?

3. How could you be more "poised under provocation" in your home, personal, and professional life?

CHAPTER 8:

THE CRUCIFIXION

Since Adam and Eve left the garden, people anxiously awaited this awful yet triumphal day. Adam was taught the law of sacrifice pointing towards this particular morning. Moses *lifted* the serpent (an early symbol of Christ) in the wilderness, symbolic of the impending crucifixion. God commanded Abraham to offer His only son in the similitude of this same heavenly offering. Countless people throughout the centuries faithfully sacrificed the unblemished lamb, symbolic of what was about to happen.

Before we get into this brutally difficult experience, let's consider some details to put the crucifixion into a better context.

First, Jesus was physically, mentally, emotionally, and spiritually exhausted. He'd been awake for nearly twenty-four hours, suffered beyond human comprehension in Gethsemane, was mocked and beaten by the Sanhedrin, lashed and beaten again by the Romans, and now stood before the people wearing a crown of thorns and sentenced to die.

Second, things were happening fast. The sun rose a couple of hours before Pilate sentenced Him, so it was sometime around eight or eight-thirty in the morning. The elders and priests were anxious and wanted this done quickly.

Third, there are two possible crucifixion sites. The most popular and widely believed site is where the Church of the Holy Sepulchre is located in the Old City of Jerusalem. The other potential site is a hill nearby the church that looks like a skull (although many scholars question this location). Both places are geographically close to one another.

Regardless of the location, the walk from the Praetorium, where He was lashed and tried, to the crucifixion site would have been relatively short — about one-third of a mile. Interestingly, Isaac was tied to an altar within a half mile of either site. Realizing these symbols, parallels, and events that the Lord perfectly orchestrated is always fascinating.

Lastly, most paintings displayed Jesus carrying the whole cross, but that's not typically how the Romans did it. In reality, they would have forced Him to carry only the crossbeam, and the vertical beam would be waiting at the crucifixion site. I was surprised to learn that the crossbeam weighed between seventy and one-hundred pounds. Understanding how heavy the beam was, makes the story even more poignant. Can you imagine how much seventy to one-hundred pounds would be on your back? Think of a time when you've done something exhausting and had no energy left (marathon, swim, bike ride, etc.). Then, consider how it would feel for someone to pile one-hundred pounds on your shoulders and ask you to walk one-third of a mile *after* whatever exhausting event you just finished. It brings some perspective to His tasks and how extremely difficult they were for Him, especially since He just endured what no other human has ever endured.

Symone of Cyrene

After the blood-thirsty mob got their hoped-for verdict, "They led him out to crucify him."

Imagine standing next to Mary, the mother of Jesus, in the crowd of onlookers while they brought out the crossbeam and attempted to lay it on His shoulders. Being completely drained and exhausted, He didn't have the strength to carry it. See if you can imagine the Roman soldiers laying it on His crimson-stained shoulders, then watching Him collapse under the weight and not be able to haul it more than a short distance. Picture Mary, with a trembling hand over her mouth and tears streaking down her cheeks, watching her bloodied Son collapse under the weight of the beam.

The Romans, impatient at the delay and seeing Jesus physically exhausted, looked for someone in the crowd to carry the beam for Him. Under Roman law, they could compel anyone to walk up to a mile. "And as they came out, they found a man of Cyrene, Simon by name: him they compelled to carry the cross" (Matthew 27:32). Though we don't know much about Simon, Mark talks about his birthplace and family, so he wasn't a total stranger. Because he was there early in the morning and Mark knew his background, he was likely a follower of Jesus.

I'd like to pause here and share my thoughts on this particular scene. My wife and I have talked about this scenario many times. If I could go back in time to be any person in history, I would choose Simon. What an incredible honor to be able to step in and physically help Jesus when He was at the point of total exhaustion. The walk to the crucifixion site is the only time in history when Jesus truly needed help and could no longer carry the load.

I'm not sure what passed between Jesus and Simon, but maybe all Jesus could muster at that point was a grateful expression on His face, or maybe He was able to utter a simple "thank you." Imagine if you were the one carrying His cross. How would you feel seeing Him lovingly make eye contact with you? How would you feel seeing Him barely able to walk next to you, doing everything He could just to put one foot in front of the other?

I consider Simon to hold the greatest honor in history – lightening the burden of our Lord in His time of need.

The Cross

It was approximately nine o'clock in the morning. After the arduous walk to the crucifixion site, the Romans took the crossbeam from Simon and laid it on the ground.

Writing about what happened next is equally as hard as Gethsemane and the lashings. It's difficult even to attempt to describe it.

Crucifixion was an awful, vicious way to die. The Romans perfected the art of pain and torture. Some of the most painful points on the body are the hands, wrists, and feet. Imagine seeing the centurions lay Jesus on the ground, pinning each arm to the crossbeam, then hammering the stakes through each palm and wrist. The pain was excruciating, and I can only imagine the groans and gasps that surely came as each stake penetrated His flesh.

Finally, they hoisted Him up, set the crossbeam in place, and hammered another stake through His feet to pin Him to the cross.

Can you imagine the pain He felt? Have you ever injured your hands or feet and felt the throbbing pain from the nerves in those areas? I invite you to pause and put a little pressure on the tendons in your wrist, rub it, and keep increasing the pressure to the point you're uncomfortable. It doesn't take much pressure to see how sensitive those body areas are.

Years ago, I was helping a neighbor move their cows. While closing the gate, I accidentally slammed the gate on my finger. It was an agonizing pain and the blood pooled below my fingernail. That night, the pain was so intense I couldn't sleep, and I woke up at one o'clock in the morning with a pulsing pain shooting through my arm. As I got out of bed and sat on the couch, I thought how excruciating the pain must have been for Jesus during the crucifixion. With this much pain in just one finger, I began to understand at a microscopic level how He must have felt when those stakes pierced the sensitive nerves in His extremities. In some small way, that moment taught me a great lesson and increased my awe for Jesus.

Despite the extreme pain, He continued to love and teach. After the centurions set the crossbeam in place, picture Him tenderly looking down on those who just nailed Him to the cross and uttering the words, "Father, forgive them; for they know not what they do (meaning the soldiers who crucified him)" (Luke 23:34).

Many prophets saw this exact moment years before and testified to it:

They will look on me whom they pierced. Yes, they will mourn for Him as one mourns for his only son, and grieve for Him as one grieves for a firstborn. (Zechariah 12:10).

And I, Nephi, saw that he was lifted up upon the cross and slain for the sins of the world. (1 Nephi 11:33).

After they nailed Him to the cross, the centurions "parted his garments, casting lots upon them, what every man should take" (Mark 15:23). Part of the humiliation of the crucifixion is having one's clothes removed to hang naked. Although paintings don't portray it that way, He hung naked from the cross, bruised and beaten.

Then, the Romans hung a superscription over His head stating in Greek, Latin, and Hebrew, "THIS IS THE KING OF THE JEWS" (Luke 23:38). What a powerful and true statement. In the twisted name of religion, the local leadership was responsible for crucifying *their* king.

Imagine standing next to Mary, James, and the other disciples looking up at Jesus – bloodied, nails holding Him to the cross, still wearing the crown of thorns, exhausted, and the pain evident on His face. Picture them crying, confused, and trying to understand how this happened.

How difficult this must have been for God the Father to watch His perfect son be pierced, despised, and humiliated. I'm in total awe of the Father as well. Maybe it's just my mortal mind, but it seemed He would have had to exercise an incredible amount of restraint not to intervene and stop this wicked, cruel torture of His only begotten Son.

Lucifer – acting through the chief priests and elders – in the moment of Jesus' greatest physical weakness, taunted Him in one final act of desperation, saying, "*If* thou be the king of the Jews, save thyself" (Luke 23:37 emphasis mine). Or, as Matthew stated, "He saved others, himself he cannot save. *If* thou be the Son of God, come down from the cross" (Matthew 27:40 – 42, emphasis mine). Lucifer uses this same age-old approach with all of us. He tries to inject *doubt* into our lives, causing us to wonder *if* we're good enough, *if* God really loves *us* and *if* we have divine potential. In this case, he taunted Jesus hoping to instill enough doubt that Jesus would succumb to his influence and come down off the cross to end His suffering.

If you were standing with the disciples and saw these Jewish leaders "wagging their heads" and mocking Him, wouldn't you feel like saying, "You've done enough. Leave Him alone and get out of here!" It would be challenging to sit back and watch their Satanic reviling.

Jesus hung there for three hours until the "sixth hour was come, and there was darkness over the whole land until the ninth hour" (Mark 15:33). Even the earth recognized that its creator, the God of nature, suffered and hung in agony. The lighting, thunder, and darkness that occurred while He was on the cross was nature's way of acknowledging what had just happened to the creator.

The Final Hours and His Death

Approaching three o'clock in the afternoon, Jesus had been hanging in agony on the cross for nearly six hours. To put that in perspective, think about how long six hours really are when a person is in that much pain. Consider timing it out. Then, imagine being on the cross for that long while the timer runs. Or think of a six-hour drive you've made at some point. When you think of it in those terms, it's easier to appreciate how long that agonizing six hours was for Him.

Finally, Jesus looked down on the mocking priests and the disciples, and with poise, conviction, and confidence, He cried out in a hoarse voice, "Eloi, Eloi, lama sabacthani!" Or, in other words, "My God, my God, why hast thou forsaken me?" (Mark 15:34). This is one of the most misunderstood declarations in history. It was far more than a plea for help to His Father. With this statement, Jesus confidently testified of who He was and boldly claimed Himself to be the long-awaited Messiah.

He had cited the opening verse to Psalm 22. Most observant Jews at this time were intimately familiar with all of the Psalms and knew the messianic Psalms by heart. Any Jew standing near the cross who heard Jesus proclaim this verse could have finished it in their mind. It's like singing, "How great thou..." and then stopping there; you could finish the words to that beloved hymn. By Jesus boldly citing the messianic prophecy in Psalm 22, He confirmed Himself as the Messiah and pointed out that they, the perpetrators, were fulfilling the prophecy.

As you read the Psalm, imagine standing in the crowd and seeing the expressions on their faces when they realized what Jesus just testified to and how it was being fulfilled:

My God, my God, why hast thou forsaken me?
Why art thou so far from helping me,
and from the words of my roaring?

O my God, I cry in the daytime, but thou hearest not;
and in the night season, and am not silent.

But thou art holy, O thou that inhabitest the praises of Israel.

Our fathers trusted in thee: they trusted,
and thou didst deliver them.

They cried unto thee, and were delivered:
they trusted in thee, and were not confounded.

**But I am a worm, and no man; a reproach of men,
and despised of the people.**

**All they that see me laugh me to scorn:
they shoot out the lip, they shake the head, saying,**

**He trusted on the Lord that he would deliver him: let
him deliver him, seeing he delighted in him.**

But thou art he that took me out of the womb:
thou didst make me hope when I was upon my mother's breasts.

I was cast upon thee from the womb:
thou art my God from my mother's belly.

Be not far from me; **for trouble is near;
for there is none to help.**

**Many bulls have compassed me:
strong bulls of Bashan have beset me round.**

**They gaped upon me with their mouths,
as a ravening and a roaring lion.**

I am poured out like water, and all my bones
are out of joint: my heart is like wax;
it is melted in the midst of my bowels.

My strength is dried up like a potsherd;
and my tongue cleaveth to my jaws;
and thou hast brought me into the dust of death.

For dogs have compassed me:
the assembly of the wicked have inclosed me:
they pierced my hands and my feet.

I may tell all my bones: they look and stare upon me.

They part my garments among them,
and cast lots upon my vesture

(Psalm 22 emphasis mine)

This was a messianic declaration. Those listening must have realized they were the malefactors and evil ones fulfilling the messianic prophecy. That had to be a proverbial arrow through their guilty hearts. In contrast to their Satanic taunts, Jesus knew who He was and that His mission was nearly complete.

Shortly after this bold, confident declaration of messiahship, I imagine Jesus lovingly looking down one final time into the eyes of His followers. He knew it was over; His mission was complete.

Then, in one final statement, He looked up and spoke the most powerful words that man might ever hear. Imagine the scene. Jesus looked up to the sky, knowing exactly who He was addressing, and cried loudly, "Father, it is finished. Into thy hands I commend my spirit" (Luke 23:46 and John 19:30).

He bowed His head at that declaration, and His mortal mission was finished. The great Redeemer died. Despite the awfulness of what just happened, while Mary, James, John, and the others were exhausted and mourning, imagine the rejoicing and celebrations in heaven. In our pre-mortal existence, what were you doing at that moment when you knew Christ successfully overcame it all? How do you think you felt when He bowed His head?

Jesus was the only one who could do it – and He did it! Though we always knew the outcome, it was now official. Satan was allowed to bruise Him during the events of the previous twenty-four hours, but when Jesus uttered those words, "It is finished," He crushed the serpent's head and sealed the fate of all those who followed Lucifer.

For anyone who followed Jesus, there was hope. At that moment, He triumphed over spiritual death. Adam and Eve, Abraham and Sarah, and every one of us knew that there was hope *because* Christ did it – He overcame death and sin.

He fulfilled all that the Father asked Him to do. There were sadness, confusion, and tears of sorrow for the followers still standing near the cross. However, there was rejoicing, hope, and tears of happiness for His followers in heaven.

Abinadi prophesied about this moment in approximately 150 BC:

And thus the flesh becoming subject to the Spirit, or the Son to the Father, suffereth temptation, and yieldeth not to the temptation, but suffereth himself to be mocked, and scourged, and cast out, and disowned by his people.

And after all this, after working many mighty miracles among the children of men, he shall be led, yea, even as Isaiah said, as a sheep before the shearer is dumb, so he opened not his mouth.

Yea, even so he shall be led, crucified, and slain, the flesh becoming subject even unto death, the will of the Son being swallowed up in the will of the Father.

And thus God breaketh the bands of death, having gained the victory over death; giving the Son power to make intercession for the children of men (Mosiah 15:5 – 8).

Post Crucifixion

When Jesus bowed His head and died, the earth acknowledged His death. The sun was darkened, and a great earthquake shook the entire region (an even larger and more destructive quake shook the Americas).

This event was so dramatic that even the Roman centurion and those nearby "Saw the earthquake, and those things that were done, and they feared greatly, saying, Truly this was the Son of God" (Matthew 27:54).

This centurion witnessed countless crucifixions but was shocked to see Jesus pronounce His death and die at His chosen time. In addition, at no other time had darkness and earthquakes accompanied the death of the person who was crucified. Therefore, imagine the realization on the centurion's face when he looked up at Jesus' lifeless body, seeing His head bowed, and understanding now that the superscription hanging over Him was correct. The centurion, feeling the heavy emotions and weight of the moment, realized and acknowledged that this man truly was the Son of God.

Just a half mile away was the Temple. This was the holy Day of Atonement – another alignment of great symbolism. It was the one day of the year when the High Priest would enter the Holy of Holies to sprinkle blood on the altar.

Today, however, the true atonement was complete. The Temple's veil "was rent in twain from top to bottom" (Matthew 27:51). In this case, the veil was rent by the Father, and the Holy of Holies was opened to acknowledge the actual shedding of blood by Jesus, the true Lamb of God. God the Father accepted His son's sacrifice and acknowledged that the scriptures were fulfilled on this day.

Thus concluded the evilest, wickedest act inflicted upon the most innocent and pure person who ever walked the earth. With total self-control throughout the whole ordeal, Jesus triumphed over spiritual death and completed His foreordained mission.

I also testify that Jesus is the Christ and the promised Messiah. At that moment, He overcame sin of every kind. We can repent and be made clean through His blood because of what He accomplished throughout His life (especially in that twenty-four-hour window). He knows us, what we're going through, and loves us beyond anything we can imagine. I am in total awe of Him and love Him more than words describe. He is the Holy One and the great Redeemer of Israel!

Reference Scriptures

Mathew 27:31 - 51

Mark 15:20 - 46

Luke 23:26 - 49

John 19:16 - 37

Prophetic References

Isaiah 53:4 – 12

Isaiah 49:16

Psalm 22:1 – 24

Zechariah 12:10

Zechariah 13:6

1 Nephi 10:11

1 Nephi 11:33

2 Nephi 6:9

2 Nephi 10:3 – 5

2 Nephi 25:13

Mosiah 3:9 – 10

Mosiah 14:5

Mosiah 15:6 – 7

Ponder, Visualize, and Personalize

Take a few minutes to visualize being there for the crucifixion. Then, while you think about that and the questions below, capture any thoughts or feelings in a journal.

1. What does His crucifixion and death mean to you?

2. Knowing what you know now, how would you have felt to be in the shoes of Simon of Cyrene and carry the cross?

3. What is one way you can express your gratitude to the Lord for all He did?

4. He sacrificed everything for us; what is one thing you could sacrifice for Him?

CHAPTER 9:

THE RESURRECTION

While the final hours of His last week are heavy and difficult to imagine, this chapter is filled with beauty, light, and hope.

For anyone who would like to study what happened between the crucifixion and the resurrection, I invite you to consider reading the apocryphal book of the Gospel of Nicodemus. It has some interesting and insightful details on what happened during that window.

As far as this chapter is concerned, five things will help us understand the resurrection better:

First, like the crucifixion, there are two potential sites for the tomb where Jesus laid. One is in the Church of the Holy Sepulchre, and the other is known as the Garden Tomb. Both are within a mile of each other. But, again, the purpose of this book isn't to discuss the scholarly analysis for each site but to focus on the experience of the resurrection itself.

Second, the four gospels vary in the details and specific order of events. So, we're left to our own interpretation and personal revelation to piece together exactly what happened and in what order.

Third, the disciples and followers of Jesus didn't fully grasp what had happened from His death to His prophesied resurrection. They didn't understand He would come back to life and appear to them. This was entirely outside the realm of possibility, making it easier for us today to understand their skepticism. Even though Jesus talked about it several times in His parables, they clearly didn't understand and weren't looking for the resurrection. John said, "For as yet they knew not the scripture, that he must rise again from the dead" (John 20:9). When it happened, His resurrection came as a complete surprise to them.

Fourth, the order in which He appeared to His followers is symbolic. He first appeared to those who were not apostles, such as those outside His inner circle who would become the newly established church's official hierarchy. This order of appearance was symbolic. It taught us that His ministry was personal and that when it came to appearing, visiting, or ministering, He was not concerned with titles. It's no coincidence, therefore, that He first visited Mary Magdalene, then His mother Mary, and next His disciples on the road to Emmaus *before* He appeared to the apostles. When He finally showed Himself to the apostles (the soon-to-be church hierarchy), He appeared first to Peter, honoring Him as the senior Apostle and, subsequently, to the remaining apostles. The primary lesson taught is the person is more important than the position.

Lastly, notice that the words sun and son are homophones – they sound the same but are spelled differently. When we remember that Jesus was the Son of God, it sheds new meaning on these homophones – both the sun and Son give light, bring warmth, dispel darkness, and give life. That morning, Mark tells us that the sun and the Son both rose simultaneously: "And very early in the morning the first day of the week, they came to the tomb when the sun had risen" (Mark 16:20). Every morning when I see the sunrise, I think of the other Son – the Son of God. God reminds us daily of His Son's resurrection.

The Sunrise and Resurrection

"The first day of the week [Sunday] cometh Mary Magdalene [and the other women to include His mother Mary] early, *when it was yet dark*, unto the sepulchre, and seeth the stone taken away from the sepulchre" (John 20:1 emphasis mine).

Did you notice they went to the tomb while it was dark? The Jerusalem sun rises at approximately six thirty in the morning in early April, so they likely arrived at the tomb around five thirty or so – which means the first hints of sunlight would be appearing on the horizon.

When they discovered Jesus missing from the tomb, they were terrified, divided up, and went different ways. Mary Magdalene ran to tell Peter and John about the missing body. This was a big deal; could you imagine the thoughts racing through their minds wondering what had happened? The apostles didn't just sit around until the sun rose; Peter and John immediately left whatever they were doing and ran to the tomb. Apparently, John was in better shape because he outran Peter. Eventually, Peter and Mary Magdalene caught up to John, and all three stood at the tomb.

Both apostles inspected the inside and found the napkin [head covering] and linens neatly folded on the stone. Still not expecting the resurrection, they weren't sure what to think, so they both "returned unto their own home" (John 20:10).

When Mary was alone at the tomb, she stood at the entrance weeping. She was heartbroken, knowing the Lord's body was missing. But as she wept, "she stooped down, and looked into the sepulchre, and seeth two angels in white. They said unto her, Woman, why weepest though? She saith unto them, because they have taken away my Lord, and I know not where they have laid him" (John 20:11 – 13).

Imagine being there for that intimate moment. Mary is standing just outside the entrance to the tomb, her eyes and cheeks moist with flowing tears. The bright, early-morning sun just crested the horizon, spreading its light on the tomb, dispelling the morning chill in the air.

Then, picture Mary turning around at the sound of a man's footsteps approaching from behind. The approaching man asked, "Woman, why weepest thou? Whom seekest thou?" Mary thought this man was the gardener and that he had taken the body of Jesus. So she responded, "Sir, if thou have borne him hence, tell me where thou hast laid him, and I will take him away." But, then, the tone in the man's voice shifted, it was the voice of Jesus, and the beautiful word flowed from His mouth, "Mary!" (John 20:15).

Can you imagine when Mary realized it was the resurrected Lord who stood before her? This was an incredible and totally unexpected reunion. One minute ago, He was lost and missing, and now He stood in front of her. Filled with joy, she ran to Jesus and embraced him, saying, "Rabboni." After a loving embrace, Jesus pulled away and told her, "Hold me not; for I am not yet ascended to my Father: but go to my brethren, and say unto them, I ascend to my Father, and your Father and to my God, and your God" (JST John 20:17).

Some translations say, "touch me not," but this isn't an accurate translation. More appropriate would be "hold" or "embrace" me not. Mary's reaction was a loving embrace, and the tears of sadness turned to tears of joy. Where once He was lost, now He returned.

Imagine the love in her facial expression, the tears of happiness, and the accompanying smile on Jesus' face – what a beautiful moment.

Mary watched Him ascend to heaven and disappear from view. Imagine the overwhelming feelings of peace and joy that swept through her. I envision her hands over her mouth, looking around, filled with excitement and awe, thinking about what just happened.

She didn't see the other disciples, so she ran to find them to share the good news of what had just happened.

While Mary ran to find the disciples, think about what was happening in heaven – the most sacred and joyful reunion ever seen. Imagine the first embrace Jesus shared with His Father (and Mother) as the resurrected Lord. What would that reunion have been like? How many tears of joy and smiles were there when they embraced for the first time after His resurrection? What a beautiful, tender, and sacred moment that must have been.

With His glorious resurrection, the sting of death was gone. Families would see their loved ones again. The chains of death were broken, and the Father's plan of happiness was in full effect. Because of that glorious morning, all will be resurrected to a perfect and immortal body.

The Other Appearances

Picture Mary, filled with excitement and joy, running back along the path to find Peter, James, John, and the other disciples. She found them in a sad and dark mood. They were mourning and weeping over the death and the apparent absence of Jesus' body. Imagine Mary bursting into the room, filled with energy, exclaiming, "He's alive. He lives. I saw Him and held Him!"

But the reaction she got from the others did not match her enthusiasm. "And they, when they had heard that he was alive, and had been seen of her, believed not" (Mark 16:11). Can you see the skeptical look on their faces while Mary related her encounter with Jesus? I can visualize them gently touching her shoulder and saying something like, "Mary, we all miss him. We all want to see him again. Maybe you were dreaming or in a trance, but let's be real, he's gone." Mary had to be frustrated at their lack of belief.

It might be easy to cast stones of unbelief at the apostles, but something like this had never happened before. No one had ever seen a person come back to life by their own will. Jesus raised Lazarus from the dead, but it was different because Jesus raised him. So if you were standing with the apostles, think about your response if someone came bursting into the room saying, "He's alive!"

At some point, Mary (the mother of James), Joanna, and other women also saw the angels who proclaimed that Jesus had risen

(Luke 24:10). As they were running back from the tomb, the Lord also appeared to His mother, if not the other women as well (Luke 24:9 – 11 and Mark 16:8). These women also came to the disciples proclaiming the good news, yet, "Their words seemed to them as idle tales, and they believed them not" (Luke 24:11).

Maybe the apostles thought, "On Friday, we saw his bloodied, torn body; how could He be alive?" But, obviously, something was going on. There couldn't be this many people fabricating the same story. They couldn't ignore the multiple witnesses.

So, hopeful and intrigued, Peter got up and "ran unto the sepulcher; and stooping down, he beheld the linen clothes laid by themselves and departed, *wondering in himself at that which was come to pass*" (Luke 24:12 emphasis mine). He was probably thinking, "Could it really be? Could He truly be alive?" Jesus then appeared to Peter. Imagine this joyful reunion. Peter, one of the most loyal and devoted disciples, had only a few days prior stood next to Jesus and smote Malchus' ear in His defense. Now, here He was, alive and whole. That must have been a beautiful moment to see Peter embrace Jesus and say something like, "Master, it's true! You've risen!"

Around the same time, Jesus also appeared to Cleopas, another disciple, and perhaps Luke, on the road to Emmaus, but they didn't initially recognize Him. These two disciples had already heard the reports of His resurrection from the women earlier that morning. While the three of them walked, this supposed stranger talked to Cleopas and Luke and taught them about the scriptures, to the point where they begged this stranger to eat supper with them. When the stranger blessed and broke the bread, their eyes were finally opened, and they saw that this man was no stranger but the resurrected Lord. They said to each other, "Did not our hearts burn within us, while he talked with us by the way, and while he opened to us the scriptures?" (Luke 24:32). They ran back to Jerusalem to share the wonderful news with the eleven remaining apostles.

Yet, even with the multiple witnesses, including Peter, Mary Magdalene, His mother Mary, and the two disciples, the remaining apostles still didn't believe (Mark 16:13).

That evening, all the apostles, except Thomas, gathered together in an upper room with closed doors. Imagine seeing the disciples huddled together discussing what would happen to them and asking questions like: could He really rise from the dead, and what should they do next? While they were talking, "Jesus came and stood in the midst, and saith unto them, Peace be unto you. And when he had so said, he showed unto them his hands and his side" (John 20:20).

Think about the astonished looks on their faces when their friend Jesus, Master and Lord, appeared to them. Picture each of them walking up to Him to see and feel the indents of the nails in His hands and feet. Imagine the feeling and emotion that swept over the room when they realized what they were experiencing. Then, Jesus tenderly rebuked them and "Upraided them with their unbelief and hardness of heart, because they believed not them which had seen him after he was risen" (Mark 16:14).

I imagine the emotions in that room shifted from initial shame for not believing to firmness and resolution. In other words, a feeling of total resolve and commitment to never again doubt Jesus (like they did earlier that day and a few days ago in Gethsemane) swept through the room. That resolve would later be tested when nearly all of them sacrificed their lives and died defending their testimony of the risen Lord.

Because Thomas was not in the room, he doubted his fellow apostles' story. He told them, "Except I shall see in his hands the print of the nails, and put my finger into the print of the nails, and thrust my hand into his side, I will not believe" (John 20:25). Doubting Thomas got what he asked for; eight days later when the apostles were all together again, including Thomas, Jesus appeared and showed him the wounds in His hands and feet.

Eventually, Jesus also appeared to a group of five-hundred and many others over the next forty days. After that, word of His resurrection must have swept through Jerusalem and Galilee like wildfire.

His parting command and counsel to each group was, "Go ye into all the world, and preach the gospel to every creature" (Mark 16:15).

The Americas

Before His crucifixion and death, He taught people by saying, "Other sheep I have, which are not of this fold: them also I must bring, and they shall hear my voice; and there shall be one fold and one shepherd" (John 10:16).

God does not favor one particular group of people and loves all His children on earth equally. Numerous legends and traditions exist among the various Native American Indian tribes of a "great God" who visited them centuries ago and promised to return. A couple of names for this legendary man are Quetzalcoatl and Viracocha.

Just as Jesus loved His followers in Galilee, He loved His followers in other parts of the world and appeared to them as well. Even though His other appearances didn't happen on the same Sunday morning as His initial appearance to His apostles, I feel it's essential to include the account here.

Below is a brief record of Jesus appearing as the resurrected Lord to the people in the Americas.

Imagine being among the American people as you read this short account. Then, imagine Him calling *you* up to feel the prints of the nails and what it would have been like to be with this group.

And now it came to pass that there were a great multitude gathered together, of the people of Nephi, round about the temple which was in the land Bountiful; and they were marveling and wondering one with another, and were showing one to another the great and marvelous change which had taken place.

And they were also conversing about this Jesus Christ, of whom the sign had been given concerning his death.

And it came to pass that while they were thus conversing one with another, they heard a voice as if it came out of heaven; and they cast their eyes round about, for they understood not the voice which they heard; and it was not a harsh voice, neither was it a loud voice; nevertheless, and notwithstanding it being a small voice it did pierce them that did hear to the center, insomuch that there was no part of their frame that it did not cause to quake; yea, it did pierce them to the very soul, and did cause their hearts to burn.

And it came to pass that again they heard the voice, and they understood it not. And again, the third time they did hear the voice, and did open their ears to hear it; and their eyes were towards the sound thereof; and they did look steadfastly towards heaven, from whence the sound came.

And behold, the third time they did understand the voice which they heard; and it said unto them: Behold my Beloved Son, in whom I am well pleased, in whom I have glorified my name—hear ye him.

And it came to pass, as they understood they cast their eyes up again towards heaven; and behold, they saw a Man descending out of heaven; and he was clothed in a white robe; and he came down and stood in the midst of them; and the eyes of the whole multitude were turned upon him, and they durst not open their mouths, even one to another, and wist not what it meant, for they thought it was an angel that had appeared unto them.

And it came to pass that he stretched forth his hand and spake unto the people, saying: Behold, I am Jesus Christ, whom the prophets testified shall come into the world.

And behold, I am the light and the life of the world; and I have drunk out of that bitter cup which the Father hath given me, and have glorified the Father in taking upon me the sins of the world, in the which I have suffered the will of the Father in all things from the beginning.

And it came to pass that when Jesus had spoken these words the whole multitude fell to the earth; for they remembered that it had been prophesied among them that Christ should show himself unto them after his ascension into heaven.

And it came to pass that the Lord spake unto them saying: Arise and come forth unto me, that ye may thrust your hands into my side, and also that ye may feel the prints of the nails in my hands and in my feet, that ye may know that I am the God of Israel, and the God of the whole earth, and have been slain for the sins of the world.

And it came to pass that the multitude went forth, and thrust their hands into his side, and did feel the prints of the nails in his hands and in his feet; and this they did do, going forth one by one until they had all gone forth, and did see with their eyes and did feel with their hands, and did know of a surety and did bear record, that it was he, of whom it was written by the prophets, that should come.

And when they had all gone forth and had witnessed for themselves, they did cry out with one accord, saying: Hosanna! Blessed be the name of the Most High God! And they did fall down at the feet of Jesus, and did worship him.

(3 Nephi 11:1 – 19)

He went on to tell His followers in the Americas, "I say unto you, that ye are they of whom I said: Other sheep I have which are not of this fold; them also I must bring, and they shall hear my voice; and there shall be one fold, and one shepherd" (3 Nephi 15:21).

What a beautiful thing to know that He not only appeared on a lovely Sunday morning to Mary Magdalene and His other followers, but He loves us all and is willing to minister to anyone who seeks Him.

His Personal Ministry

It happened to others; imagine it happening to you. From doubting Thomas to the women who loved Him to His followers in the Americas – He appeared and taught them all.

He invites us all to come unto Him, to see and experience what others have experienced. This chapter focused on His resurrection and appearance to others, but let's make it real to you.

Imagine the Lord appearing to you (it doesn't matter what setting you visualize). Picture His beautiful eyes looking into yours, filled with love, compassion, and understanding. Imagine Him saying what He said to the disciples, "Come, feel the prints of the nails in my hands and feet."

At that point, I would kneel and bathe His feet with my tears of joy and gratitude!

Imagine Him, regardless of what you've done, sweeping you up in a loving embrace with a smile on His face. Everything you've done and beat yourselves up over would be swept away by His all-encompassing love!

At this moment, I invite you to pause, set the book down, close your eyes, and take however long you need to visualize that experience. Just focus on being present and searching your thoughts and feelings.

Then, in the coming months and years, if you continue to focus on that personal relationship with Him and anxiously seek Him, what you're visualizing in your mind will eventually become the real thing.

Many others through the centuries have proclaimed, Jesus is the Christ, the resurrected Lord, and He will return – that is also my witness!

Reference Scriptures
Mathew 28
Mark 16
Luke 24
John 21

Prophetic References
Isaiah 25:8
Isaiah 26:19
Mosiah 3:10
2 Nephi 25:13
1 Nephi 10:11
2 Nephi 26:1
Mosiah 16:7
Mosiah 16:8
Alma 11:42
Alma 33:22
Alma 40:16

Ponder, Visualize, and Personalize

Take a few minutes to visualize being there for the various resurrection appearances. Then, while you think about that and the questions below, capture any thoughts or feelings in a journal.

1. What does His resurrection mean to you?

2. When you think of the day when you will be resurrected with a perfect body and reunited with your family and friends, how do you feel?

3. How can knowledge of the resurrection help you replace fear with faith?

4. How will you feel when you get the opportunity to feel the prints of the nails in His hands and feet?

CONCLUSION

I hope your relationship with Jesus Christ is stronger, deeper, and more personal than when you started this book. And if you didn't have a relationship with Jesus Christ, I hope this book accurately described what He did for *you* in His final days.

When we visualize and ponder these experiences and imagine being there to witness these different events, they become more real and personal. In this manner, the Lord can reveal new insights and help us see things differently – not just from what we read, but from what He can reveal through personal revelation.

When I think about His final week, it demonstrates how much He loves us. The more I learn about Him and understand Him, the more I'm in awe of Him.

If visualizing and pondering these experiences positively impacted your life, I invite you to come back and read this book each year (especially around the Easter season) and reflect on the questions and your answers at the end of each chapter. Additionally, if there is someone you think would benefit from reading this book, please consider sharing it with them.

While we prepare for His return, He's looking for people committed to Him, ready to stand for truth, and willing to defend His name. You wouldn't be reading this book if you didn't love Him. So, thank you for your commitment to His work as we prepare together for His great and glorious return.

I'll finish with my witness that He lives! There is no greater treasure than to experience His infinite and all-encompassing love. Despite the many times we fall and make mistakes, He is *always* there to pick us up. There will come a time, whether in this life or the next, when every knee will bow, and every tongue confess that Jesus is the Christ!

ABOUT THE AUTHOR

Rob was born and raised in Orem, Utah. He served a two-year mission for the Church of Jesus Christ of Latter-Day Saints in La Paz, Bolivia.

After his mission, he graduated from Utah State University and earned an MBA from Colorado State University. After that, he spent 11 years as a fighter pilot in the United States Air Force. During his time in the Air Force, Rob was also an Air Force One Advance Agent.

Rob is the CEO of Becoming Your Best Global Leadership and the author of several books, including *Do What Matters Most, Start with the Vision: The Six Steps to effectively plan, create solutions, and achieve your goals; Conquer Anxiety; Return and Succeed: 12 powerful habits for success after your mission,* and *A-Z: The Best in You and Me* (a children's book written with his daughter Bella).

While Rob loves training people and organizations worldwide, his greatest passion is his love for the gospel of Jesus Christ.

He was blessed to be born into an amazing family. Unfortunately, in 2020, his mother passed away from early-onset Alzheimer's. While he misses her deeply, he looks forward to the day they (along with his family) will be together again because of Jesus Christ and His atonement.

Rob currently lives in Heber City, Utah. He's been married for 24 years and has four wonderful children.

Made in the USA
Coppell, TX
22 March 2024

30444063R00072